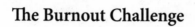

The Burnout Challenge

THE BURNOUT CHALLENGE

Managing People's Relationships with Their Jobs

Christina Maslach and Michael P. Leiter

HARVARD UNIVERSITY PRESS

Cambridge, Massachusetts

London, England

2022

158.7

First printing

Library of Congress Cataloging-in-Publication Data

Names: Maslach, Christina, author. | Leiter, Michael P., author.
Title: The burnout challenge : managing people's relationships with their jobs /
Christina Maslach and Michael P. Leiter.
Description: Cambridge, Massachusetts : The Belknap Press of Harvard
University Press, 2022. | Includes bibliographical references and index.
Identifiers: LCCN 2022001811 | ISBN 9780674251014 (hardcover)
Subjects: LCSH: Burn out (Psychology). | Industrial management. |
Success in business.
Classification: LCC BF481 .M3845 2022 | DDC 158/.7—dc23
LC record available at https://lccn.loc.gov /2022001811

We dedicate this book to all those people who told us their stories,
shared their experiences, answered our questions,
and thus shone a bright light on burnout.

Contents

The Burnout Challenge

Introduction

Across most of the twentieth century, in coal mines around the world, miners took caged canaries underground with them to test the air quality. The canary's high sensitivity to carbon monoxide and other toxic gases meant that, if it swayed on its perch, or even collapsed, the coal miners were forewarned in sufficient time to get out.

The practice was ended by the 1990s, but to stretch the metaphor let's say our hope was to keep more birds singing in mines. What would be our best approach? Should we try fixing the canary to make it stronger and more resilient—a tough old bird that could take whatever conditions it faced? Or should we fix the mine, clearing the toxic fumes and doing whatever else necessary to make it safe for canaries (and miners) to do their work?

In recent Gallup polls, majorities of American workers rate their jobs as mediocre or bad.[1] Globally, the situation is even worse, with only 20 percent of employees reporting that they are engaged with their jobs.[2] A recent study of British citizens found that, when they were working at their job, their happiness dropped around 8 percent relative to their average happiness in other life activities. The only thing they associated with more unhappiness than working was being sick in bed.[3]

Apparently, for entirely too many people, work is an unpleasant place of cynicism and despair, and something to be endured rather than a source of satisfaction or pride. Our own research has included many conversations with a broad spectrum of workers about their workplaces. Here are comments representative of the discontent and frustration we've heard:

From a physician: "I gave 110 percent for many years only to find myself exhausted, bitter, and disillusioned. If I could do another profession with my medical degree, I would. I would advise my children to avoid medicine."

From a tech worker: "I love my work. I am an avid learner and a very positive person. But I work in a socially toxic workplace. This is a highly political environment that encourages competition between colleagues, backstabbing, gossiping, and hiding information. I find going to work very difficult and I come home exhausted."

From an engineer: "A large problem is that the company is always moving in new directions, and this is done in secret without receiving input from the professionals who actually perform the jobs. It makes us feel devalued when changes are made to a department or program, but the staff is never consulted or asked what could be done to improve their job."

There is a paradox here. Organizations' ideals and employees' experiences are disconnected, even at odds with one another. At a time when leaders extol the virtues of respectful workplaces and engaging teamwork, complaints of incivility, abuse, and bullying run rampant. Even as consultants and managers incessantly beat the drum of engagement, dissatisfaction remains an intense concern, including in the professions offering the greatest possibilities for vibrant, dedicated, absorbing work. Everywhere, there are thoughtful leaders deeply concerned with helping their employees be productive, fulfilled, and healthy—and there is proof that some of what they do makes a difference. But the evidence also shows that, all too often, their efforts fall short of the mark.

Various social, political, and economic factors have shaped the work environment such that many jobs are increasingly stressful. Competitive pressures to cut costs and increase profits have resulted in downsizing, for example, leaving smaller staffs to manage the same workloads. In some sectors, changing public policies—and in health care, the rise of managed care—have strongly affected what customer-facing workers can provide and what they cannot. For many kinds of work, real wages have declined, and job benefits have been cut back. The result is a fundamental contradiction in the workplaces of the twenty-first century. On the one hand, organizations increasingly need the creativity and involvement of their employees. On the other hand, organizations have made changes that undermine people's capacity to be engaged in their work.

Burnout

The negative impact of these workplace trends creates an employee experience of a crushing *exhaustion,* feelings of *cynicism* and alienation, and a sense of *ineffectiveness*—the triumvirate known as *burnout.* The burnout syndrome occurs when people experience combined crises on all three of these dimensions, most of the time. They feel chronically exhausted; they have withdrawn mentally, socially, and emotionally from their work; and they have lost confidence in their capacity to have a constructive impact. Basically, this means that they are experiencing high stress, a hostile job environment, and a pessimistic evaluation of themselves. Burnout is an apt term, suggesting a once-hot fire that has been reduced to ashes: those ashes are the feelings of exhaustion and a lack of engagement left after an initial, internal flame of dedication and passion is extinguished. The accelerants are the workplace conditions creating too-hot environments and leaving behind this trifecta with its scorching effects on people's lives.

Burnout is also not a new term. Indeed, it has been part of the popular vocabulary for the better part of a century, and perhaps even longer. (Google's Ngram viewer charts its rise from a starting point in the 1820s.) The concept of the human stress response to difficult life events (stressors) was developed in the 1950s.[4] Before then, burnout (or burn-out) was most commonly used in engineering to describe the result when repetitive stress or excessive load on a piece of equipment ruins its ability to function (as when a motor, or light bulb, or rocket booster burns out). Perhaps the engineering use of the term was why its application to workplaces took off in Silicon Valley, where early start-up ventures were referred to as "burnout shops." But burnout also became a slang word for a chronic drug abuser and resonated with the idea of "burning the candle at both ends." Graham Greene called his 1961 novel about an architect in a state of spiritual crisis and disillusionment *A Burnt-Out Case.*[5]

By the 1970s, workers in various realms of health and human services were using *burnout* to describe their own job crisis. One of us (Maslach), conducting interviews with such workers for a research project, heard the term repeatedly along with the stories behind it—and soon shifted the project to focus on burnout instead.[6] She collaborated with Susan Jackson in 1981 to publish the Maslach Burnout Inventory (MBI), an instrument for assessing the experience. Then the two of us (Leiter and Maslach) joined forces on three lines of work: developing additional versions of that measurement tool and a new one, the Areas of Worklife Survey (AWS); conducting research studies on burnout with international colleagues;

and writing our first book on burnout.[7] Since the latter came out in 1997, we have conducted studies in numerous organizations, tracking the development of job burnout, finding ways of reversing it, and nudging people toward engagement instead. Clearly, understanding burnout has been a major focus of our lives' work. In this book, we pull all of it together into an integrated perspective on burnout and what to do about it.

In 2019, the World Health Organization (WHO) recognized burnout as a legitimate occupational phenomenon that could have a negative impact on the well-being of workers in the workplace.[8] In its words:

> Burn-out is a syndrome conceptualized as resulting from chronic workplace stress that has not been successfully managed.
>
> It is characterized by three dimensions:
>
> - feelings of energy depletion, or exhaustion.
> - increased mental distance from one's job, or feelings of negativism or cynicism related to one's job.
> - reduced professional efficacy.

The year after WHO recognized burnout as a legitimate occupational phenomenon, the coronavirus disease—abbreviated as Covid-19—forced the closure of many workplaces, including offices, schools, restaurants, food-processing facilities, and more. Starting in early 2020, the pandemic caused many people to experience dramatic changes in their job, often with no warning or preparation—just think of the healthcare workers whose workload increased with the onslaught of Covid patients, or the teachers suddenly educating students online rather than in person. Other people had to deal with the uncertainty of cutbacks in their organizations, and risks of losing their jobs entirely.

We already knew that, when workplaces are designed mostly for the economic bottom line, they may miss the mark on the human one, and that they can actually be *bad* for the people who work within them. Many decades of research on various risk factors in the workplace (such as high demands, toxic hazards, job insecurity, lack of control, and so on) have shown that unhealthy job environments harm employees both physically and mentally, with ultimate damage to the economic bottom line.[9] The pandemic added even more risk factors to this equation—such as working too close to other people, for longer hours, in enclosed spaces.

During the pandemic people were using the term *burned out* colloquially to describe feeling stressed. Doing so does not question burnout's research-based definition, any more than people saying colloquially that they are depressed challenges the reality that depression is a clinically diagnosable condition. But it was in the midst of this challenging time that we felt, more than ever, that we needed to share a deeper understanding of burnout and how to combat it, based on decades of research and analysis of data.

Mismatches in the Workplace

We believe burnout arises from the increasing mismatch between workers and workplaces. As the WHO definition explains, the occupational phenomenon of burnout is the result when chronic workplace stressors have "not been successfully managed." If conditions and requirements set by a workplace are out of sync with the needs of people who work there, this bad fit in the person–job relationship will cause both to suffer. Our research has identified at least six forms of mismatch that can exist between a job and the person holding it:

- work overload
- lack of control
- insufficient rewards

- breakdown of community
- absence of fairness
- value conflicts

Poor alignment in any one of these six areas increases the risk of burnout. For example, let's consider work overload. If job demands cannot be met within the usual workday, then employees have to work extra hours and take time away from other important parts of their lives (such as personal interests, family and friends, and sleep). We've found that these bad mismatches often have their roots in erroneous assumptions about what makes people tick—what motivates them, what rewards them, and what discourages them. In other words, there is often a misunderstanding of basic psychology. The more that any or all of these six conditions depart from employees' aspirations or preferred ways of working, the more employees are vulnerable to burnout.

In the chapters that follow we detail these six mismatches—what they are, why they have such a toxic effect, and how to fix them and achieve better matches between the job and the person. If mismatches can be corrected or improved, then there are ways to prevent burnout and promote greater engagement with work.

The analogy we began with of the canary in the coal mine is an apt one for understanding the burnout experience, because it focuses our attention on three critical things: the individual, the context, and the relationship between them. If the individual canary is noticeably suffering within the context of the mine, it is a red-flag warning that the context has problems—that will affect not only the canary, but any other individuals working there. One could say that the relationship between the canary and the coal mine represents a serious mismatch between the individual (with its need for oxygen) and the workplace (with its carbon monoxide–filled air). What can be done, for the individual and the workplace, to fix the relationship between them, so that work can be done safely? The answers lie in the pages to follow.

PART I

The Marathon

1

Working in the Burnout Shop

Calling a business a "burnout shop" was a popular phrase in the early days of Silicon Valley. It was an exciting time in the tech boom. New start-ups were formed, money was flowing, and companies needed to hire workers. Companies' want ads even bragged about their reputations as burnout shops. The hours would be long (the concept of 24/7 was invented here), the work would be challenging, and everyone would have to sacrifice a lot of their personal lives for this particular quest. After a few years, employees would burn out—but even if they were unable to work anymore, they would leave with some promising stock options in a fledgling business.

Working in the burnout shop was like an all-out sprint, with people going as fast as they could under extreme conditions.

What characterizes the burnout shop of today? To put it simply, the sprint is now a fast-paced marathon. The short-term strategy of self-sacrifice and speed has become the long-term operating model for many businesses. As one consultant put it, "Everyone's job is now an extreme job."[1] But running at a sprint pace cannot be sustained over a long period; it leads to debilitating consequences such as ongoing stress experiences, physical exhaustion, sleep deprivation, poor job performance, and disruptions of personal and family life. The mismatches between people and their jobs have been getting even worse.

Workplace Stressors

Some might say that dealing with stress is a common part of everyday life, whether at work or home or anywhere else. So what is the problem here? Just what goes on in burnout shops that makes them especially stressful? The answer lies in two characteristics of the stressors they commonly present. First, a workplace stressor typically involves a serious *mismatch* (or imbalance, or bad fit) between the person and the job. Second, the stressor is *chronic*—it causes stress repeatedly, perhaps every day, for reasons that are difficult to change. Chronic stressors take more of a physical and psychological toll on people than do occasional stressors (such as unanticipated challenges or emergencies, when everyone must jump in to do more than usual to fix the situation). When chronic stressors also involve mismatches, the result is erosion—a wearing-away of one's ability to cope effectively, to be involved in one's work, and to take pride in one's achievements. These everyday stressors may be little things, such as rude or sarcastic comments from fellow workers, or bureaucratic processes that are tedious or disruptive, but their erosive effect over time can be considerable. Six chronic mismatches in particular combine to shape the characteristic features of the burnout coal mine.

WORK OVERLOAD

The burnout shop is an "always-on" work culture, where job demands are high and continue to keep piling up, and resources necessary to meet those demands (such as time, tools, goals, support) are often insufficient. In many of today's companies, the explicit directive to "do more with less" is demoralizing and confusing, and undermines employees' energy, involvement, and competence. It is no surprise that many people compare this experience to that of Sisyphus, the Greek mythological character who was condemned for eternity to push a boulder up a hill only to have it roll back down just before it reached the top. Despite their hard work, people are not sure they are making any meaningful progress.

In many cases, increasing workloads demand people's efforts beyond the traditional boundaries of work hours. If the work cannot get done on time in the workplace, then employees may have to work overtime, or take work home to finish it there, or even take on extra job tasks to get the project completed. In other words, "Overwork happens." A culture of working long hours assumes that productivity rises when salaried employees spend more time at work—especially as "people deliver under pressure." There is not, however, much support for this assumption. Instead, much evidence shows links between working long hours and illness, as well as lower productivity.[2]

Especially dispiriting to people is having their plate overfilled with tasks that are not a match for their capability level and that do not contribute to their strengths at performing the job they were hired to do. In medicine, for example, physicians have invested heavily to gain their expertise and are most happy working extra hours if they are "working at the top of their license"—that is, performing the highest-level services they are qualified to render. Administrative busy work—like populating electronic medical records—is bottom-of-the-license work. Tasks like this, and equivalents in other jobs—like generating reports that no one reads and completing online training modules unrelated to one's work—fall into the category of "illegitimate tasks" that people resent doing.[3] Workers are required to accomplish these tasks within regular work hours, but they experience them as a burden, or a drain on the time and energy that they could be devoting to more important work. An irony comes when managers (who normally champion an on-task focus) must enforce policies that divert employees' finite energy to trivia.

For many, the workday is stretched further by a commute that keeps getting longer. Housing close to urban workplaces has become increasingly expensive while wage stagnation has constrained the amount of money people have available for housing. Housing prices outstrip the capacity of people to pay because urban properties have become investment vehicles supported by vast pools of wealth searching for attractive returns on investment. Housing supply remains tight due to zoning constraints in many places. Across a recent five-year period, the number of "super-commuters" (those commuting more than ninety minutes each way) rose by 40 percent in ten US states.[4] That time feels more like "work" than leisure, and people are not getting paid for it.

This expanding workload often comes with personal costs, as reflected in oft-heard complaints like "no work-life balance is fostered," and "unpaid overtime is expected." Employees may be reluctant to say no to requests to do extra work because they fear they might not be promoted, or might be demoted or shut out of opportunities, or might even lose their jobs. Feeling they have to work more hours, even when "off-duty," puts strain on their personal lives. It erodes their relationships with family and friends, and harms their health and well-being. As one hospital worker we know told us, "There is a culture of high stress in our department due to high workload, which results in a constant high anxiety and low mood. This impacts staff morale. The level of high stress and anxiety for me personally has resulted in significantly high levels of sick leave for myself, and high medical bills. I have been thinking about leaving the workplace as a result."

The boundary between work and home was greatly eroded during the Covid-19 pandemic, which forced many people to "work from home" rather than leave their home to do their job in another place. The hours devoted to their jobs—as opposed to the rest of their lives—became blurry, in terms of both the numbers of hours and when they took place during the day or night. There were reports of people devoting even more hours to work when they were at home than when they had been in the workplace. For some, this was a response to a period when they saw others losing jobs. As the pandemic wore on, people were more afraid for their own livelihoods and worked harder to stay employed.

Workload is not just about hours, however. An even more important aspect can be the emotional burden involved. This is especially true for healthcare and human services providers, as well as first responders, who deal with patients and clients under very emotionally stressful conditions. The emotional labor inherent in such work can intensify especially when caseloads expand. This burden became overwhelming during the pandemic, when healthcare workers faced the need to care for huge numbers of severely ill Covid-19 patients while trying to avoid getting sick themselves and bringing illness home to their families. Some had the heartbreaking experience of keeping families away from loved ones and being the only people with suffering patients when they died. Many doctors, nurses, and others who have worked many years in health care have said that they have never felt so burned out in their lives.

This speaks to another factor contributing to a work overload mismatch beyond sheer volume of work and its emotional toll: a heavy workload is more exhausting when someone does not have the capacity or opportunity to recover and bounce back. Without effective, ongoing recovery processes, people only become increasingly tired, worn out, and unenthusiastic about going back to the job the next day. An executive coach we know works with high-tech leaders under enormous pressure at their companies. "Good athletes," he observes, "have learned how to turn on their stress hormones and respond when they absolutely have to, then release and relax. But in Silicon Valley, the stress response is turned on all the time, even when stress is not there."

LACK OF CONTROL

The burnout shop is often characterized by problems in power dynamics, such as micromanagement, incompetent leadership, and ineffective teams. Too often, people are denied the necessary autonomy to do their jobs well, sometimes by being excluded from critical decisions relevant to their work. Feeling ignored, limited, manipulated, distrusted, and undermined brings greater uncertainty and frustration to their daily work-lives. People feel fear and anxiety about doing their work correctly and potentially being punished (even demoted or fired) for getting things wrong. At the same time, they feel angry, resentful, and alienated being constantly second-guessed, overruled, and shut out of any efforts to improve or innovate. Workers who do not have an appropriate amount of autonomy over the work they do, who are unable to make choices and exercise discretion to do it well, simply do not feel effective in their jobs.

Also constraining and limiting individuals' control and options are often situational factors. For example, in occupations focused on direct interaction with clients or patients, the sheer number of people with whom an employee must engage can be overwhelming. When the patient or client load becomes too great, quantity compromises quality. People no longer have the option to provide the level of service or treatment they would choose to render—especially as time limits tend to be imposed, such as "no more than fifteen minutes per person." As the attention and effort allowed for each case is minimized, workers can succumb to callous, even cynical, "processing" of clients or patients. Consider the situation of lawyers doing legal-aid work. "I have so often seen good, competent lawyers begin to process people like machines, rarely doing more than placing their problem into a category to be recorded and mechanically dealt with," one worker reports. "I have watched the same attorneys lose their enthusiasm, their creativity, and their commitment. People are dealt with and described in statistical terms, in general rather than in particular, and as part of a stream of problems rather than as human beings."[5]

Health care is famously a profession in which high patient loads, along with stepped-up requirements for digital record-keeping, have left many physicians feeling like mere cogs in a machine over which they have no control. Educators also tend to be responsible for many people, at all levels from elementary schools to universities. One college instructor described how heavy workload translates to diminished autonomy: "The experience of burnout is different from simply feeling fatigued or exhausted; it typically stems from a lack of perceived control that leads people to feel overwhelmed and 'at the end of their rope.'"[6]

Beyond autonomy in specific job tasks, workers also want to feel they have control over their schedules and earnings—and many have lost ground here, too. Even if they have agreed to work extra hours, they may find themselves unable to take compensatory time off to regain the personal time they lost. Wanting the predictability of a reliable schedule, some instead see their (and their family members') lives disrupted by work hours that shift from week to week, or by needs to respond to unanticipated work needs on short notice. For many, the unsettling sense of not being in control of income and work hours was greatly exacerbated during the Covid-19 pandemic.

Where workers feel a lack of autonomy, often that sense is a relative one—a contrast with a level of independence they used to have—and often the culprit is a new manager. After a restructuring of a hospital's organization took place, an employee complained about the rising burnout on her team: "This is not a gripe about that restructure—however, it is a reflection on how this individual chooses to manage the team, ignoring the way the team prefers to work, which is predominantly fixed in a culture of respect, authenticity, and collaboration. The new manager's style does not allow for this collaboration, autonomy, or freedom—nor is there allowance for diversity of thought, or the space for error or disagreement." She described the dispiriting atmosphere the team now experienced: "What prevails is an autocratic *do as I tell you*, divide-and-conquer mentality. Every aspect of the work is micromanaged, and the person spends hours reworking the written work done by team members or others in the organization, and even those external to the organization." Clearly, bosses in organizations have power invested in their positions and are expected to exercise authority, but if the manner in which they do this creates chronic feelings of lack of control, they not only damage efficacy but also engender cynicism. Their actions signal a lack of faith that others around them believe in the organization's mission and know how to advance it.

INSUFFICIENT REWARDS

In burnout shops, people often feel they are not reaping sufficient rewards—financially, socially, or emotionally—for the hard and high-quality work they are doing. Of course, for many, the most important rewards are the intrinsic ones that come with making progress in meaningful and challenging work. They become frustrated and depressed to the extent that their jobs bog them down in trivial tasks and discouraging cases or projects. But extrinsic rewards matter, too, and many experience their pay as too low, benefits as too few, and promotions as too infrequent. They feel unrecognized and underappreciated, believing their accomplishments are routinely ignored, even when they have gone above and beyond what was needed. Positive feedback is rare, while negative feedback may be plentiful. Indeed, when asked to describe "a good day" on the job, many workers reply, "When nothing bad happens." Evidently, having "something good happen" is too rare or unreasonable to expect. Living with such a low standard for one's daily experience reflects frustration and disappointment, and provides little motivation to do one's best work.

Sometimes to provide a desirable reward an organization decides to set up a contest, or generally promote rivalry among the staff, on the assumption that competition will motivate everyone to work harder and better. Competition, however, also sends other messages. One is that employees succeed by defeating each other, which prioritizes individual gain over collective benefit. Another message is that there can be only one winner and all others are, by definition, losers. As an example, during the Covid-19 pandemic, most schools and colleges switched from teaching students in person to teaching them online. This unexpected change had to be enacted instantly, which called for enormous efforts by course instructors to quickly revamp their teaching methods, become adept in using unfamiliar technologies, and learn how to deal with students attending classes and taking tests remotely. It was a huge challenge that required long hours and hard work to maintain teaching excellence and deliver it successfully. At one school, instructors received an announcement requesting their nominations for a set of distinguished teaching awards during the pandemic. This attempt to name a few among them as "best" was not well received. "Why can't the school do something that recognizes all of us," one asked, "like a letter of thanks or some small gift of appreciation? Why does recognition have to be a competition, which will leave a lot of us with bad feelings, because we are not as valued?"

At times, social rewards are lacking simply because people are so overloaded by work that they forget to give positive feedback or to thank each other for working longer and harder. In some settings, however, their absence reflects a mistaken belief that the best way to motivate people is with negative reprimands, penalties, and punishments. In fact, positive reinforcement can be far more effective.[7]

BREAKDOWN OF COMMUNITY

In burnout shops, the always-on culture of fear is particularly damaging when it poisons people's relationships with their coworkers. Instead of viewing their colleagues as supportive and trustworthy, people may come to suspect that they are surrounded by people "only in it for themselves" and willing to do anything to get ahead. Under such conditions, they do not seek out advice or help, lest they reveal a weakness that could be used against them. Thus, work environments allegedly designed to win the race to success and innovation can actually undermine the effective collaboration and teamwork required for these. The system pushes people toward their worst behaviors—selfish actions at the expense of others' well-being and the organization's mission.

Any workplace can be vulnerable to the bad behaviors that take place in the society around it. Workers can be targeted, for example, by racist and sexist remarks if their colleagues harbor such prejudices. But the always-on intensity and exhaustion of burnout shops make it more likely that antisocial behaviors will erupt, go unchecked, and lead to community breakdown. These behaviors can occur at all employee levels of the organization. Sometimes they occur between team members, or among staff with similar jobs or positions—and they often involve things like name-calling, making sarcastic remarks, talking behind a colleague's back, or trying to belittle or intimidate one's colleagues. Such behavior among peers has been described as horizontal violence.[8] It is not always clear what the reasons are for horizontal violence, but it has been argued that when people are stressed and oppressed by the system in which they are working, and feel unable to fight back against those constraints, they may relieve the tension by striking out at members of their own group.

Consider two very different realms in which such horizontal violence can be seen. The first is among the community of social activists, who work passionately in support of humanitarian causes (such as promoting peace or fighting climate change) but earn little for doing so, and are at risk for burnout because of this dedicated commitment and sacrifice. When seventy-five such activists were surveyed about the rewards and stressors of their work, the intriguing finding was that "relationships with other activists" proved to be their most common reward *and* most common stressor.[9] A comment by one sheds light on how resentments can arise: "I feel overwhelmed, and sometimes I look at the stuff I have to do and I get angry. Like, why doesn't somebody else do some of this stuff? Why is it just me? And I begin to think that other people don't have the same dedication."[10]

The second example is from tech workers in the field of cybersecurity, who struggle with huge work overloads and have no control over when security incidents will suddenly occur and how long it will take to respond. There are too few people working in this area—the number of unfilled positions is enormous. Yet, a big part of the problem, people in the field are now realizing, is that even when workers are recruited into these positions, cultures of horizontal violence drive too many away. Exhaustion combines with what one industry insider described as a tendency toward "egocentric, gatekeeping territoriality" to cause veterans to be hypercritical and dismissive rather than supportive of their newly hired colleagues. And therefore the exhaustion of their heavy workloads continues.[11]

Sometimes uncivil social behavior is not laterally directed but comes from the top, from bullying bosses. One executive coach describes this as "red-ink behavior" because a manager's tirades, needling, and intimidation lead to lost productivity and financial losses.[12] This kind of management style is often associated with other disruptive interpersonal behaviors, such as being unsupportive and quick to assign blame after a failure has occurred, having difficulty responding to critical feedback, and not working well with others. It may be that some of these leaders are suffering their own burnout, and their reaction to the experience is sowing the seeds of burnout all around them.

Whether they come at people horizontally or vertically, toxic encounters are exhausting. They prompt intense emotions that linger physically and mentally through rumination well after the event. They undermine the sense of psychological safety, deny people a sense of belonging, and undermine core values. Even when other mismatches are not in play—say, workloads are reasonable and autonomy is high—community breakdown in a workplace can, on its own, push people toward burnout.

ABSENCE OF FAIRNESS

The burnout shop is often an unfair place—decisions are viewed as unjust, people are not treated with respect, and various processes and outcomes are biased and discriminatory. Unfair treatment marks its targets as lacking legitimacy in the community, excluding them from full membership, and injustice can move directly to exploitation. Working under such conditions, employees quickly develop a high degree of cynicism.

A sense of unfairness is an important offshoot of power dynamics. Critical decisions about the distribution of rewards and punishments, tasks and priorities, and individual career tracks have direct implications for people's ability to manage their workloads and potential to do meaningful work. Decisions by powerful individuals or groups often are made outside of most employees' control.

Concerns about fairness often focus on favoritism—perceptions that the CEO or the managers like some people and dislike others. Those seen as favorites may appear to be pandering to the boss's ego in illegitimate ways. Those who are targets of scorn may seem to have been singled out because they raised concerns in the past, or have personalities or opinions different from the boss's. In either case, employees perceive that key decisions are shaped by personal likes and dislikes rather than objective evaluations of merit.

More extensive injustice arises from systemic biases built into the structure of workplaces, their policies, and their practices. For much of recorded history in many parts of the world, race and sex explicitly determined eligibility for high-status positions. By now, legal sanctions and social norms have for the most part banished such explicit discrimination, but workplaces still fall well short of fair access to opportunity. One dynamic arises from the implicit biases individuals bring to decision processes. These were revealed, for instance, in a now-famous study of the effects of "blind auditions" for symphony orchestras. When screens were installed so that juries listened to performances without seeing the players, the proportion of women advancing through the process and ultimately hired by orchestras increased significantly. Removing cues as to the candidates' demographic qualities eliminated the role that unconscious biases about male versus female musicians had been playing in the choices and focused evaluators completely on the auditory experience.[13]

Beyond individual biases, unequal treatment (including pay discrimination) can result from organizational norms and expectations of how people prove themselves in their jobs. In a company, for example, that prides itself on the royal treatment it provides to demanding customers, it may be a prerequisite for a position that an employee always be available to jump in whenever and wherever needed by a client. Yet women in the workforce are more likely than their male counterparts to have family responsibilities that demand predictability or flexibility in their work hours. Such clashes between what companies and some employees prefer and need result in constrained opportunities. Thus, considerations that make no explicit reference to gender or other attributes can still block access to higher-status positions, cutting off the pathways to top positions on boards and executive teams.[14]

VALUES CONFLICT

In burnout shops, people's relationship to their work can also be undermined by values conflicts, especially when job requirements clash with moral principles. An employee may feel compelled to do something unethical, such as tell a lie (to make a sale, or get a necessary authorization, or cover up a mistake). Sometimes an organization itself has conflicting values, preaching one thing while practicing another. For example, it may emphasize the imperative to be customer-centric ("we always do what serves the customer best") but, in a challenging quarter, instruct salespeople to push certain products as much as they can, regardless of whether they are the best fit for a customer's need. Or it may call work-life balance a core value, but promote only employees who travel extensively or work over weekends. Often, multiple values are declared to be fundamental, but are to some degree incompatible, leaving people unclear on which takes priority.

Typically, the kinds of values that the most dedicated employees bring to their work are antithetical to the values system of a workplace focused on maximizing profitability or fending off short-term threats to survival. In all too many situations, people under pressure do things that feel wrong to them because those actions serve their employers' objectives—accepting that morally corrosive philosophy that the ends justify the means. If the mismatch between what their values dictate and what they feel compelled to do is large, then the potential for burnout is high.

A workplace does not have to be morally bankrupt, however, for there to be a mismatch between its requirements and the values of an idealistic employee. We saw this, for example, in the case of an emergency medicine physician who chose to leave her job in a community hospital. She had previously spent a six-month deployment in an Afghanistan combat zone, which she described as her most fulfilling professional experience, despite the long hours and horrific injury cases. It was only when she came back to practice at the community hospital that she experienced burnout. The work felt meaningless, "rinse and repeat," and she could barely get out of bed in the morning. "I was turned off by the extremely toxic environment and the corporatization of health care delivery." She felt like a cog in a machine, whose only value to the hospital was to earn money—and that wasn't why she had gone into medicine. Eventually, she quit her job to work in the emergency room at a children's hospital where, despite a pay cut, she has more flexibility, fewer hours, and a work environment in which patient care is paramount. A key factor: Physicians are treated as valued professionals, she says, "not worker bees."[15]

Most employees do their best work when they believe in what they are doing and their daily work nourishes their integrity, pride, and self-respect. When they feel they have morally capitulated to workplace values in conflict with their own, they often describe this as an "erosion of my soul"—a sense that they have actually lost some of their own integrity, dignity, spirit, and will. When highly paid employees quit their jobs, even despite offers of more money or other benefits, it is this "soul erosion" that is pushing them away.

Understanding Mismatches

These six areas of job-person match or mismatch are not independent of each other, but can overlap in multiple ways. For example, when overtime demands are not optional, a workload mismatch links to a control mismatch. When salaries are frozen but the boss's favorite gets a bonus, a rewards mismatch is compounded by a fairness mismatch. Thus, there are many ways in which mismatches can combine. Meanwhile, the reciprocal interactions among coworkers over time mean that every individual can be affected by mismatches and also contribute to mismatches for others.

A way of thinking collectively about these six areas is to note that, together, they capture the three essential dimensions of a person's relationship with their job. One of these is the *capability* dimension— and this is usually the first one that people think about (and sometimes the only one). It consists of the first two areas of job-person match discussed above: workload and control. Workload, again, refers to the degree of manageable demands and sufficient resources, while control refers to the degree of autonomy and opportunities for influence. But there are two other dimensions that are just as important, and sometimes even more salient to the risk of burnout. The *social* dimension consists of its own two areas of job-person match: reward and community. Recall that reward refers primarily to social recognition and positive feedback for a job well done, while community refers to the social culture of the workplace and the social relationships between the people who are employed there. Finally, the *moral* dimension consists of the last two areas: fairness and values. Fairness refers to the presence of respect and impartial processes in the workplace, while values are central to the meaning of one's work and the integrity of the organization. Each of these dimensions of the person-job match deserves some focused discussion.

THE CAPABILITY DIMENSION

This dimension is the one that most people think about when they think of burnout: "There is too much work for me to do, and I do not have enough say in how I can do it well." On the surface, burnout can seem like the simple outcome of heavy demands at work. People become exhausted from having too much to do. Although this captures some of what is happening, it misses a lot, as well. Sometimes people with the most tasks to accomplish in an organization are doing fine, while colleagues with smaller caseloads or less urgent demands feel distressed. There seems to be more going on than a straight line from heavy commitments to exhaustion. When asked whether more job demands lead to more distress, people have tended to answer, "It depends."

The development of the Demand/Control model, a framework for analyzing risk of job stress, enabled important progress in figuring out what else was going on.[16] The model highlights the key importance of another variable: workers' control over how their work is done. Situations with high demands and low control lead to distress. But situations with high demands and high control do not. People's level of control at work can rise as they gain skills, strategies, help from others, autonomy, equipment, supplies, or any number of resources that help them manage the demands placed upon them. The model clarifies that the driver of distress is not so much workload per se, but *unmanageable* workload. The World Health Organization statement on burnout, with its reference to "stress that has not been successfully managed," points directly to this juncture of workload and control.

Focusing on control as well as workload defines the challenge of preventing burnout as an organizational management issue rather than a personal health issue. Evidence that an employee is experiencing chronic stress should not always lead to a personal treatment plan. Instead, it should prompt efforts to develop more general strategies for improving workers' relationships with the workplace. Certainly, urging employees to work harder does not constitute a meaningful or helpful response.

THE SOCIAL DIMENSION

The quality of people's connections with others in the workplace is critical to their sense of belonging to a good community. People function best when praise, comfort, achievement, help, humor, and happiness are shared with others they like and respect. When their job-related relationships are functioning well, employees benefit from a great deal of social support, have effective means of working out disagreements or problems, readily exchange recognition and appreciation, and are more likely to experience engagement. In fact, being a valued member of a team is rewarding in itself, quite apart from the team's accomplishments. All of the social rewards and recognitions available at work depend on people to convey and share them.

By the same token, when workplace relationships function badly, the social atmosphere turns toxic, tainted by unresolved conflict, incivility, disrespect, hostility, social isolation, and even ostracism. That kind of work environment fosters greater distress among the workers, raising the risk of burnout. Although negative social encounters are not the only causal factor involved, promoting a more positive social environment can significantly improve people's experiences in the workplace.

Research on burnout has always recognized the central role for social relationships in the development and resolution of the syndrome. Initially, as research focused on burnout in various health and social service occupations, the emphasis was on the therapeutic relationship between the provider and the service recipient.[17] Over time, studies have confirmed that relationships with colleagues and supervisors are equally, if not more, relevant to a worker's potential to experience burnout. In a reciprocal way, workers experiencing burnout can have negative impacts on their colleagues, both by causing greater personal conflict and by disrupting job tasks. Thus, burnout can be "contagious," spreading and perpetuating itself through social interactions on the job.[18] Negative social interactions seem to drain people's energy and to distance them from their jobs, and the absence of positive social encounters is discouraging. Such findings suggest that burnout should be considered a characteristic of work groups, rather than simply an individual syndrome.

THE MORAL DIMENSION

People do their best work when they believe in what they are doing and when they are being treated fairly. These considerations make up the moral dimension of the match between the job and the person. By moral, we mean what is good and ethical and fair. To say that someone has a strong moral character is to call that person a good member of society. When we talk about people of moral responsibility, we mean they reliably do the right things—not just for some people, but for all those whose lives they impact. People who act with integrity are often described as having a moral compass, which guides them to know right from wrong and to proceed accordingly.

But what happens when good people are working in an environment that is not so good? Fairness plays a pivotal role in the moral domain, as workers constantly assess how they are being treated and how they see others being treated. Suppose there is a gap between what is preached and what is practiced, or when employees have to sacrifice the quality of their work to meet quantity targets? Suppose there are pressures to behave in unethical ways, or there is bias and discrimination against them?

In healthcare professions, there has been a longtime concern about *moral distress*—a response that arises when one knows the right thing to do, but institutional constraints make it nearly impossible to pursue the right course of action.[19] More recently, this phenomenon has been described as *moral injury* or *compassion fatigue*, both of which result when, say, hospital workers are torn between doing what they know is the right thing for patients and obeying efficiency-minded hospital rules. Or when first responders must deal with highly traumatic incidents without the resources they need to help victims.

The latter problem was pervasively felt during the Covid-19 pandemic, when communities everywhere faced shortages of personal protective equipment for healthcare workers, hospital beds, and vaccines. Pandemic responses in some places raise yet another ethical issue, which is "employee silence."[20] In many occupations, including health care, pressure can be put on employees to keep quiet about any negative issues in the workplace, even when those involve hazardous, unethical, or illegal matters. Not only does an imposed norm of employee silence have bad effects on organizational performance, it takes a physical and psychological toll on the people who feel compelled to suppress their thoughts and emotions in the workplace.

The moral mismatch in such situations can be huge and can lead to the kind of soul erosion that is perhaps the epitome of full-blown burnout. Remember the emergency physician described above? Her experience of burnout was not so much a feeling of exhaustion or inefficacy. It arose from a mismatch in values, as she saw her life's purpose as helping injured people, whether soldiers or children, and resented feeling that her efforts were being directed more toward making a bureaucratic institution more profitable. We have seen such moral mismatches play out in other professions, as well. Always, they involve people questioning the value of what they are doing and the price it is exacting from them—as they trade health for wealth, for example. In one of the most famous verses of the Bible's New Testament, Matthew 16:26, the question is posed: "What good will it be for someone to gain the whole world, yet forfeit their soul?" In some cases, people decide to quit their jobs, and when they give notice they are offered larger salaries or other benefits to tempt them to stay. And for some of them, the response is, "No thanks, I would rather keep my soul."

Mismatches and the Canary

The conditions in burnout shops pose real hazards for the employees who work in them. Like coal mines where the air has turned toxic, these are environments that are unhealthy and unsafe. We see this in the six areas of mismatch, which represent the most dynamic points of connection or disconnection between people and their jobs. But if a workplace is a burnout shop, or turning into one, how can that be assessed? How can we determine when conditions are safe enough for human beings to spend their time working there?

The solution for the coal mine was to take a canary into a section where miners were working and pay attention to how well it functioned. Used as a kind of assessment tool, the bird would indicate if there were problems with the mine's environment. It was just a single, individual canary, but its reaction to low oxygen in the air could be interpreted as evidence of what could happen to any other living creature that remained in the mine, too. In many of today's workplaces, however, an individual worker's distress is misinterpreted as a problem with that individual. Solutions are focused on fixing the worker rather than the workplace. As we will see in the next chapter, there is much more to learn from the individual worker— the canary in the burnout shop.

2

Sounding the Alarm

The canary in the coal mine has interesting parallels to the worker in the workplace. Burnout functions like an invisible but toxic threat that afflicts some in an environment sooner than others. Like the canary, a person experiencing burnout could be considered a harbinger, a sensor sounding an early warning that something is going wrong more generally. To resolve problems of burnout, we must heed the canary's distress and investigate, with both the mine and the canary in mind.

For a catalog of classic red-flag signals of burnout, consider the case of Stan, a psychologist in his third year of employment as a therapist in a community mental health center. In just that short time, he has seen himself "change from an avid, eager, open-minded, caring person to an extremely cynical, not-giving-a-damn individual." At the age of twenty-six, he has developed an ulcer. To relax enough to sleep at night, he has used alcohol and taken tranquilizers. He has used up all his sick days. To get through the rest of the year, he is resolving to be less emotionally invested in his crisis intervention work, and instead to approach it "as if I were working at GM, Delco, or Frigidaire." He might as well adopt an assembly-line mindset, because "that's what it has become here, a mental health *factory!*"

Stan describes arriving at the slow and painful realization that he needs time away from constantly dealing with other people's sorrows; things have reached the point that he starts shaking upon entering the office. "That's it," he says. To head off the deadness that is beginning to spread inside he will have to ask for a leave of absence. "It hurts to feel like a failure as a therapist in terms of not being able to handle the pressure, but it's better that I do something about it now, rather than commit suicide later after letting it build up much longer."[1]

Stan's account is not atypical among people who have had full-blown experiences of burnout. You may recognize a friend in part of his story—or yourself, even if you work in a very different field. A valuable outcome of our early publications on burnout was exactly this. We heard from many whose reaction was, "That's just how I felt! I know what burnout is because it happened to me, too!" In the letters and phone calls that followed, we learned their personal stories and perceived how important it was for them to get this kind of validation of their difficulties. Another message came through strongly, as well: "All this time, I thought it was just me, I was the only one, some sort of unique freak. Now it turns out there are others who have experienced it, and there is a name for it." Spreading the word that "other people experience burnout, too" began to normalize the experience—certainly not as something good or desirable, but as something that was more common and widespread than people knew.

What Is Going On with the Canary?

Our own approach to understanding the individual experience starts with the Maslach Burnout Inventory (MBI), a research measure we scientifically developed over the course of years. The MBI assigns scores to three dimensions: exhaustion, cynicism, and inefficacy.[2] People report the frequency of their experience of these dimensions, which might be on the high end (every day, or a few times a week) or on the low end (a few times a year or less, or never). They are asked, for example, to rate statements such as "I feel emotionally drained from my work" and "I don't really care what happens to some recipients."[3] The extensive research that has been done with this measure, by us and by many other researchers around the world, has yielded important insights about burnout—including, importantly, confirmation that it is defined by these dimensions. Burnout is not a simple feeling, or outcome of a single factor, but a complex mix of exhaustion, cynicism, and inefficacy.

The first dimension, exhaustion, which is the individual stress response, is often the first sign that a person is having a problem with their job. This measure includes physical and mental components. People feel overwhelmed by work demands and depleted of the necessary resources to meet them successfully. They feel drained and used up, without any source of replenishment and recovery. They lack enough energy to face another day or another problem. The exhaustion experience is also described by such terms as depletion, debilitation, fatigue, and feeling worn out.

The second dimension, cynicism, refers to a negative, callous, or excessively detached response to various aspects of the job. It can develop in reaction to the overload of exhaustion and can be self-protective at first—providing an emotional buffer of "detached concern." If people are working too hard and doing too much, they will begin to back off, to cut down, to reduce what they are doing. But the risk is that the detachment can result in the loss of idealism and the dehumanization of others who are the recipients of their services. Over time, workers not only create buffers and cut back on their quantity of work but also develop negative reactions to their jobs and the people they encounter in them. The cynicism experience is sometimes called depersonalization (given the nature of human services occupations), but other words and phrases used to describe it include irritability, withdrawal, loss of idealism, compassion fatigue, and generally negative and inappropriate attitudes toward clients. As cynicism develops, people shift from trying to do their very best to doing the bare minimum.

Inefficacy is the third dimension, and it refers to feelings of powerlessness and a lack of achievement and productivity in work. Any position holder has a sense of *self-efficacy* in their job, which is their own belief in their capacity to do it well. When they are hindered by insufficient job resources, social supports, or opportunities to develop professionally, their self-efficacy suffers. They may feel they have made a mistake in their choice of career path, or are turning into a kind of person they dislike. As people develop such negative regard for themselves, as well as for others, they lose more confidence and may sink into depression. Inefficacy has also been called reduced personal accomplishment, incapacity, low morale, and inability to cope.

We must make an important distinction here: burnout is chronic, not occasional. To feel exhausted in the morning once in a while, or to sometimes be frustrated by a workday with no real accomplishments to speak of, is just part of normal life. But feeling exhausted day after day and almost never feeling effective at work are indications of a chronic condition. In workplaces full of stressors, people are likely to experience the dimensions of burnout frequently at work, rather than a few times a year.

Over years of studying individuals in such situations, we've learned that burnout can lead to other personal consequences. People often report health declines, including more frequent illnesses, chronic fatigue, sleep disturbances, musculoskeletal pain, and cardiovascular problems. They talk about negative lifestyle changes— losing sleep, skipping meals, exercising less, falling into bad habits involving smoking, alcohol, or drugs. By making it harder to do a good job, burnout undermines self-confidence and further erodes job satisfaction. Workers feel their jobs having negative effects on their home lives and may experience anxiety, depression, or loss of self-esteem. They try to minimize their time at work, or simply quit, preferring financial loss over further damage to their physical and emotional health.

Prolonged stress, fatigue, and frustration can lead a person to worry openly about what is going wrong: "Why can't I handle this? What should I do about it?" It can also lead some people to vent frustrations and treat colleagues in cynical, hostile, or demeaning ways. Most often, however, such feelings are not shared explicitly; the cynicism and inefficacy that come with burnout are more typically hidden from others. Meanwhile, the exhaustion that comes with it may be visible—but viewed in positive terms, as a sign of "giving one's all." Even well along the path to burnout, a person might see it as a source of pride and reason to brag, "I'm tough enough to take anything."

Blaming the Victim

Burnout often comes with a stigma. It is viewed as a sign of weakness, failure, and incompetence, no matter how or why it occurred. This stigma means that burned-out workers fear they will be treated more negatively by supervisors or managers or coworkers—for example, receiving poor job evaluations, being passed over for pay raises or promotions, being "thrown under the bus" by colleagues, losing their jobs, and so on. These are not unrealistic fears. In years past, it was not uncommon for company leaders to view burnout as a useful phenomenon: it meant that people who couldn't cut it would quit on their own, saving managers the bother of firing them. When we first began our research decades ago, the stigma attached to burnout posed some challenges for getting accurate information, and it has never completely disappeared.

Today, many employees report that a "culture of fear" within their workplaces means that they can never say no when a boss asks them, for example, to come in to work on a day they were scheduled to

have off, or take on a task with an unreasonable deadline, or work late without overtime pay. Workers subject to a culture of fear do not speak up or tell the truth about problems with their jobs, or suggest ways to make things better. The belief is that such comments will be interpreted as whininess or evidence of personal weakness, and that this negative judgment ("clearly, you are not working at 100 percent") will cause one to be demoted in various ways.

In recent years, awareness has grown about an inordinate number of suicides among young men working in the tech start-up sector. One senior tech leader who had known one of these men and admired his talent and ability posted a heartfelt account on an industry blog sharing his dismay that he had been unaware of the man's distress and did not know to try to help him. He described later reaching out more to fellow tech workers when there were signals they were struggling, urging them to call him if they ever got close to thinking like that.[4] Later, at a tech convention, his comments were referenced from the stage by a speaker who exhorted anyone in the crowd suffering from burnout to do the same: "Reach out to someone, anyone, at work when you feel the need for some help!" There was a silent pause, and then hands started to go up, and people pushed back on the idea that it could ever be that easy. "Well, that sure sounds nice, but I tried reaching out, and it really does not work," one said, "because other people will judge you as stupid and weak and a loser, and just put you down." Others agreed, saying that "they don't want to have anything to do with you," or that, at best, colleagues might say, "Just fix yourself up, and then when things are better, we can have a beer, okay?"

For people with burnout, the challenge of seeking help is compounded: not only are they stigmatized for having the problem in the first place, but it is assumed that fixing the problem is also their own responsibility. The judgment is that burnout is dispositional—which is to say, it results from a person's natural tendencies as an individual. If someone needs help, the cause of the problem lies within her or him. The attitude of "if you can't take the heat, get out of the kitchen" exemplifies this belief. This amounts to blaming the victims, and even shaming them, perhaps in an effort to push them out of the workplace.

Perhaps for these reasons, to protect themselves from its follow-on consequences, many people try to hide burnout. But suppressing one's thoughts in a social setting can trigger a phenomenon known as *pluralistic ignorance*, in which members of a group for the most part believe something but each of them pretends not to, because their misperception is that the rest believe otherwise. Pluralistic ignorance, in other words, always involves major misperceptions of social reality. In the case of a work group beset by stressors, any individual burned-out person, if convinced that no one else is having that experience, may hide it from public view, put on a happy face, and hope that no one will notice. But if others are doing the same, then everyone has a happy face—sending the false message that "we are all doing fine." Individually, each receives that false message and is reinforced in thinking "I'm the only one!" Interestingly, in our burnout studies with employers, when results have been shared with participants about the overall organization or their unit within it, they have often been shocked. Hearing, for example, that "56.3 percent of you said you have become more callous toward people since you took this job" has been an eye-opening moment, when people start looking around at each other, stunned to learn so many others answered as they did.

This effort to manage one's public emotions, to prevent negative social judgments, occurs in other forms, as well. For example, people may put aside their commitment to personal values to convey allegiance to work group or organizational values—adopting what is known as a *facade of conformity*.[5] In some settings, masking one's true emotions is actually part of the job, a component that has been described as *emotional labor*. As examples, consider flight attendants, expected to keep smiling and being nice even if passengers are rude or unruly, and healthcare personnel and first responders, trained to project calm and compassion even in the midst of crises (as seen in abundance during the pandemic).[6] Essential to doing the job well is learning to display certain emotions (surface acting) or to really feel certain emotions (deep acting). It requires real effort and energy expenditure, however, to deliberately evoke or display emotions that aren't naturally felt, or to suppress ones that are. Where this is required, it constitutes another risk factor for burnout.

Searching for Solutions

As we have just seen, experiencing burnout can attract negative attention from other people and can lead to further negative consequences. Not surprisingly, workers are often reluctant to self-identify as having this problem or needing help, given that positive outcomes seem unlikely. Thus the individual experience of burnout can easily progress to become intense and debilitating.

So, what are the potential approaches to alleviating this kind of personal suffering? In the case of the canary, one response is to recognize the toxicity of the coal mine, remove the bird from it, and take actions to restore it to full health before taking it back in. Likewise, with human workers, many coping strategies involve removal from the workplace (through leaves, vacations, or reduced hours) and improvement of well-being (through rest, relaxation, healthy habits, and exercise). But another response is to view burnout as an unusual inability of the individual to tolerate an atmosphere that others do not find toxic—in other words, as a sort of illness or "medical" condition that needs to be diagnosed and treated or cured. Both of these responses—the coping strategies and the medical approach—assume that the problem lies within the worker, and that the solution is to "fix" the worker in some way. They're both akin to making the canary better and healthier and stronger, so that it won't be bothered by the conditions in the coal mine, which will not be altered.

Based on extensive research, we strongly disagree that "fixing the person" should be the focus in dealing with burnout. We argue instead that burnout results from mismatches between the person and the job, and that solutions must therefore address *both* the workers and the workplace. To be sure, there are many ways in which individuals can take action to improve a situation for themselves, and we support the use of better coping strategies. But encouraging the use of coping techniques is very different from trying to "cure" a case of burnout. To understand why, it is useful to evaluate why this medicalized approach has taken hold as a dominant perspective on the problem and how it leads to misplaced priorities.

THE MEDICALIZATION OF BURNOUT

By now, conventional wisdom has shifted to the position that, if a person has a burnout problem, it should be taken seriously as a health issue that needs to be fixed in that person. The push to medicalize burnout as a form of disease has included efforts to define identifiable symptoms, consistently diagnose cases, and specify effective treatments or cures. There is no comprehensive body of evidence, however, to support the idea that burnout is a disease. The World Health Organization states, in fact, that burnout "is not classified as a medical condition," and refers to it instead as an "occupational phenomenon" that deserves attention because it can influence a person's health status and decision to contact health services. The burnout experience may be linked to health issues that can be diagnosed and treated (such as cardiovascular problems or depression), but this does not mean that it constitutes a disease in its own right.[7] Similarly, the American Psychiatric Association, which oversees the criteria for mental illnesses as classified in its *Diagnostic and Statistical Manual of Mental Disorders,* has rejected the inclusion of burnout in that manual on the grounds that it is inherent to the human condition and not a psychiatric disorder.[8]

Given that there is no substantial body of clinical evidence to support the idea that burnout is a personal disease or disability, why have there been ongoing efforts to medicalize the phenomenon? A major rationale has been that doing so places burnout within existing systems of disability and health care, with their well-established mechanisms for legitimate health problems to be treated by healthcare professionals and to be paid for by health insurance companies. There are noble goals involved here, to help burnout sufferers access services and enable skilled helpers to provide assistance. But this proposed solution is based on changing the fundamental concept of what burnout is. Essentially it is an expedient compromise, saying that "if the only legitimate way for a person to gain help in solving their problem is that they have a medical condition, then burnout should be defined as a medical condition."

It should be noted that the medicalization of burnout can have the positive effect of directing greater attention to employees' overall health and well-being. Promoting a healthier workforce pays off in many ways, including less absenteeism and sick leave, fewer negative health impacts on colleagues, clients, and customers (such as the spread of infectious diseases), and greater energy, engagement, and resilience. Many organizations have made changes to enhance worker health, such as providing exercise equipment or fitness classes on-site, putting healthier food choices in the vending machines, offering special classes to stop smoking or lose weight, and so forth.

One problem, however, with the medicalization of burnout is the emphasis it puts on the problem of formal diagnosis. Some workplaces resist this, believing it is enough for an employee to self-identify as someone having a problem with burnout. These employers recognize that burnout is a real possibility and accept that an individual reporting problems with it deserves some help and support. Typical actions taken in response to such individual pleas include leaves of absence, shortened work weeks, job rotations, changes in job tasks, referrals to personal coaches or therapists, and early retirement plans. The basic idea is to listen to the particular challenges the person is describing and devise a tailored course of action to help them. Taking a customized approach to employee well-being is not a brand-new concept. Indeed, highly individualized professional development and support is fairly common for people in the upper echelons of organizations—often referred to as the top talent—if not for the rank and file. To the extent that an organization wanted to enhance the well-being of all its employees, the same personalized approach would prove effective.

The more common hope in organizations, however, is that burnout could be diagnosed with a more "official" test based on accurate measurement of telltale symptoms. Much like a thermometer is used to identify a fever, or a blood test to reveal cholesterol levels, a test for burnout would ideally provide a score indicating if the person is a burnout case, and if so, how serious their case is. The scores yielded by such a test would be informed by sufficient medical research to establish the test's validity and reliability. In reality, as noted above, there is no body of clinical evidence on which to base a medical diagnosis, but that has not kept popular desire for a standard, objective test from growing. Organizations and the people they look to for expertise often devise alternatives to serve that same function. In many cases, they simply repurpose questionnaires or other measurement tools designed by researchers to study the burnout phenomenon (including the MBI). They then translate ranges of scores on these research instruments into greater or lesser levels of burnout and treat these as true medical diagnoses.

To some degree, the desire for such a test emanates from individuals: a person may be worried about emotions they are feeling and want to know if it could be burnout, or they may have a partner, friend, or colleague they think could be motivated by an objective test to make some healthier lifestyle changes. The demand, however, comes more powerfully from organizations increasingly focused on employee well-being, who would find it valuable to have a reliable mechanism for identifying burnout cases in need of attention. There is ample evidence of such "burnout tests" being incorporated into annual surveys of worker populations and their findings being treated as viable metrics of workforce well-being. As the surveys are repeated on a regular basis, managers pay attention to whether the collective average scores show improvement over time or decline. In this way, test scores are used to diagnose burnout at the level of entire populations rather than just the level of the individual worker. If such surveys are answered anonymously (as is usually the case), then the test scores can only function as an overall metric, serving to answer the question of "What percentage of our workforce is burned out?"

Given the stigma associated with burnout, anonymity is a concern—and not always properly safeguarded. Even when a survey does not ask for a name or employee number, for example, it may ask for information such as the respondent's role, organizational unit, or demographic characteristics, which together would make it easy to deduce their identity. This raises both ethical concerns and also practical ones, if fears of being found out lead to self-censoring in responses. In some cases, surveys are designed not to be aggregated but to produce individual-level findings, and this also raises issues. It is one thing if that personal score is kept confidential and shared only with the employee for purposes of self-understanding. It is another thing, however, if a burnout score is delivered to the employee with specific information about what to do, such as get medications, get therapy or counseling, "shape up" and do better work, or find another job. And still other problems come up if an "imposed" diagnostic test of burnout, which the person did not request and perhaps was unaware of, is shared with others. For example, here is what a medical student had to say about being surveyed:

> Each year we have to answer questions about how our medical training is going. And if we answer honestly about the stress we are going through, and the huge patient load, then we get tapped on the shoulder by some supervisor who says, "Hmm, looks like you are having a personal burnout problem, so you had better go see a psychotherapist about that." And we know that any of us who have a "problem" will not be getting good grades or a good letter of reference for an internship, so why jeopardize ourselves? And of course, we know that nobody is going to do anything about the patient load. So we just lie, and say things are fine, even if they are not.

There are other ways in which the confidentiality of diagnostic test scores can be violated. We have even heard reports from health-care workers of names and burnout scores having been posted publicly on bulletin boards or in entranceways to workspaces. It is hard to imagine the rationale for doing this; perhaps it was to encourage some mutual support or motivate team-level changes, but it seems more like a way to shame individuals.

Similar confidentiality lapses can arise when organizations have "wellness committees" or employee advocates such as ombudsmen to whom workers can go to seek help for burnout and other concerns. Of course, such support services can be a positive source of advice and comfort for troubled employees. But too often there is insufficient assurance of privacy. Once the worker confides in another, will that information be kept secret, or will it end up becoming somehow known by other colleagues? Is one's record going to become more public? In some cases, others can see who goes into the designated service office, so that the very decision to use the service is not private. (We once saw a police station where the psychiatrist's office was located right next to the police chief's.) Under these circumstances, the "take rate" for such services can be low.

Beyond anonymity concerns, people in organizations can resent filling out surveys that provide no insight to them. No matter what a survey asks or the answers might reveal, the question should be asked: Will aggregate findings be shared with all the employees, given that they have contributed to them? Our general impression, developed over many years, is that the people behind these tests and surveys often do not share their data and analysis very widely. Neither are people informed about how the information is used by organizational leaders and what changes are prompted by it. We routinely hear complaints from employees that they are often asked to spend time answering survey questions but never see the results. The following comment is typical:

> Every year we get asked to answer the same set of questions about our jobs here, maybe a few new ones, but mostly the same old, same old. The first time we did this, I really took it seriously and answered as best I could. And in the last section, which asked for suggestions on how to improve things here, I spent a lot of time writing about what I thought would really make a difference. And I know a lot of the other people in our unit did the same thing, as we would talk about what we had written. So we waited to hear what management thought about all this. And waited and waited . . . and got nothing, truly nothing, beyond some vague BS about "working on it." There was never any acknowledgment that they had even read what we had written or had any opinions about any of it. And then, the next year, we were told to fill out the same survey again. Really? So I just

whip through it as fast as possible. Wait again. Again, nothing. A year later, the same survey, same questions. Forget about it! I just threw in some random answers, other people refused to fill it out at all. Just adds to the cynicism that the leaders at the top don't know what is really happening here and don't want to hear from us.

At the same time, we hear complaints from organizational leaders that their surveys are not working well. There can be many reasons for this, ranging from problems with what metrics are chosen and why, to poor implementation of the survey process, leading to low response rates and untrustworthy data. Perhaps most often, however, managers become frustrated because "the needle isn't moving"—they are not seeing declines in burnout, or increases in engagement, or some other hoped-for improvement. Often the real culprit is a lack of meaningful follow-through on what the surveys revealed. The evidence that results from everyone's responses must be used in some productive ways. What does management see in the data, in terms of either positive or negative indicators? How does this information point to potential improvements? The overall goal to improve the health of all employees, and thereby promote the success and well-being of the larger organization, is certainly something to applaud. But administering a test through a required annual survey is hardly enough to achieve that goal.

All of this is not to say that such assessment techniques of the workforce as a whole are not a good idea—they can indeed be a valuable source of relevant information for future improvements. But they have to be carried out correctly and with integrity. And they must yield actual benefits. If nothing of value ever emerges from these repeated tests, then it is no wonder that people end up grumbling about "survey burnout," and the process deteriorates into a useless exercise in "garbage in, garbage out."

The larger point, for purposes here, is that uses of standard questionnaires and survey instruments to gauge levels of burnout reinforce the sense that it is a diagnosable condition in individuals who should then be expected to seek cures. Even as such efforts reflect a positive emphasis on worker health, they leave the individual worker likely to be blamed for burnout. We have received numerous accounts of people who were "diagnosed" with burnout and then given prescriptions for tranquilizers and sleeping pills, or who were required to get some form of psychotherapy for their personal shortcomings. Even the helpful "What can we do for you?" is often heard as "*We* are fine, but *you* are not." As with other forms of mental distress, such as sadness, depression, and anxiety, a burnout diagnosis is still highly stigmatizing, viewed as a sign of personal weakness or failure. The common opinion that burnout is one of these "bad" characteristics makes people afraid that, if others find out that they are "mentally ill," more bad things will happen to them. Many would rather deny that there is any problem at all than reach out for help, even when they recognize they need it. This is why we recommend the alternative focus discussed next: equipping individuals with coping techniques rather than offering "cures."

INDIVIDUAL COPING TECHNIQUES

What can one do, on one's own, to feel better and work better? The basic answer is that individual people can indeed learn how to cope more successfully with job stressors. This approach differs from that of the burnout medical diagnosis in two ways. First, it does not make any assumptions about whether the person is the cause of the problem; the cause is independent of what coping techniques might be used. Second, it does assume that the individual has the capability and the competence to learn new skills and develop new strategies for coping with sources of stress. The inherent message is one of personal autonomy and potential—"You can do it!"—rather than the stigmatizing message of "You can't help it." In recent years, this individual approach has been given a new name of *resilience*. Originally used to describe some objects' ability to spring back into shape after being stretched or bent, the term now refers to a person's ability to recover quickly from difficulties or stressors, and thus to "bounce back" from adversity.[9]

The range of possible coping techniques is vast—and there is clearly a massive self-care industry eager to teach people how to use them. Given all that is already available in so many forms (books, online materials, videos, classes, and coaching sessions), there is no possibility here to survey that landscape in detail. But we do want to offer, in summary form, an overview of what this field of coping entails.

Most of the ideas proposed for coping with burnout are not new—they are strategies drawn primarily from previous work on stress and health, which are considered equally relevant to the burnout experience. They fall into seven main categories of advice, each of which includes many variations on its main theme.

Stay healthy. The healthy person, being likely a stronger and more resilient person, is better able to weather any stressor storms, and there are many things one can do to improve and maintain one's health. Eating healthier foods, both on and off the job, and eating regularly are important. This means cutting down on "junk" foods, drinking more water to stay hydrated, and not skipping meals. Exercising regularly also contributes to good health and can be done before or after work, as well as during work breaks—whether that means walking, jogging, biking, working out on fitness equipment, taking fitness classes, or playing sports with others. Altering behaviors that increase the risk of developing chronic health problems is another important strategy, which could involve quitting smoking, losing weight, and other healthy moves.

Get enough sleep. A critical part of staying healthy is getting enough sleep and rest. This means seven to eight hours of sleep within a twenty-four-hour cycle, whether overnight or with the help of brief naps when needed. Especially helpful are strategies for winding down and preparing to rest, so that one sleeps well and deeply and awakes refreshed and restored.

Relax. Relaxation strategies help offset the tension of experienced stress by reducing high arousal and inducing a state of calm. There are many ways to do this, ranging from meditation and mindfulness to massages and music. Some relaxation strategies are intended to be used on the job, whereas others focus on how to relax after the workday is finished. A relaxed lifestyle also includes nonwork-related activities and hobbies, which can provide the kind of quiet peace and tranquility that are a positive counterpoint to the agitation and turbulence of work.

Understand oneself. Raising one's level of self-awareness—becoming more conscious of one's own personality, needs, and motives—can enable personal adjustments and coping responses. People with greater self-awareness are more likely, for example, to modify their job expectations to be more realistic. They might recognize that their strong desire to be appreciated by others is making it too hard to say no. They might recognize some negative tendency in their behavior, perhaps being too quick to say things that strike others as inappropriate or hurtful, and therefore learn to pause and count to ten. There are many ways to achieve new levels of self-knowledge, either on one's own or with the assistance of professional counselors or therapists.

Develop new skills. Becoming more competent in one's specific job tasks can improve how one responds to work stressors. So can building related skills, such as in time management and conflict resolution. There are also, however, skills that can be learned directly relating to stress management. Acquiring the skill of *cognitive restructuring*, for example, involves learning to recognize stress-producing thoughts and then deliberately replacing them with thoughts that will not have that effect. Similarly, one can build greater capacities to imagine new goals and next steps, interpret the meaning of others' behaviors, or clarify one's values. Learning to share emotions more productively with colleagues can both reduce tension and lead to better understanding of sources of frustration and success.

Get away from the job. One of the most common recommendations for coping with workplace stressors is a simple one: "work less!" This can mean taking breaks from work, slowing down one's pace of work, avoiding overtime, taking "mental health" days off, and enjoying restful vacations. It can also mean going on a sabbatical, taking a leave of absence or medical leave, or arranging a permanent reduction in hours worked per week. A related recommendation focuses not on reducing work time per se, but on making more of one's nonwork time. Doing more to enforce boundaries makes it more likely that stress from the workplace will be eased by more benign conditions in the rest of one's world. The question of how to set work-nonwork boundaries took on new importance during the Covid-19 pandemic, when many people had to shift from working in offices, schools, and other facilities to working from home.

Get social support. Most of the time, it is not enough to try to beat burnout alone. Other people of all kinds can be critical and valuable resources for those struggling to cope with workplace challenges. Professional support from colleagues, effective guidance from supervisors, and kindness and love from family and friends—all are helpful. Reaching out to others is the key to gaining direct assistance, emotional comfort, new insights, and social recognition. It provides reassuring bases for comparison and prevents depressing social isolation. Friendly connections are also a much-needed source of humor, optimism, and encouragement when the going gets tough.

Within all of these categories, the good news is that there are lots of coping strategies to choose from. But there is some downside to the variety, as well: research studies on which individual strategies are most effective in reducing the risk of experienced burnout have shown mixed results, so there is no clear winner when it comes to defeating burnout.[10] A given technique might work better for some people than others, and different techniques may be more or less appropriate and relevant to different jobs. Some may be easier to access, perhaps because they are made available to workers as part of their job benefits; for example, growing numbers of organizations offer yoga classes on-site and provide counseling resources. Other strategies may require more individual initiative to pursue—and involve more individual expense. In the end, there is no single "magic bullet" for all situations, or guaranteed "best practice" for everybody at all times.

Beyond Burnout

Do all workers experience burnout? *No.* Do some workers have other work experiences? *Yes.* But to draw the conclusion that the world can therefore be divided into two groups of workers—those who are burned out and those who are not—would be simpleminded. To understand the more complicated reality, it is useful to see every individual's experience as constantly being shaped by and responding to negative or positive changes along three dimensions. One dimension is their *individual effort* on the job: at any given time, this falls somewhere on the spectrum from giving up in exhaustion to diving in with energy. The second dimension is their *social context* on the job, which can range from distant cynicism toward the rest of the organization to close involvement with colleagues. The third dimension is their *self-evaluation* on the job, landing at some point between a shamed feeling of professional inefficacy and a highly positive sense of successful accomplishment.

The pattern for burnout is made up of frequent negative "scores" on all three dimensions—but obviously this is not the only way an employee can score. There are individuals who land in positive territory across all three dimensions, providing models of "how things can go right." Instead of feeling exhausted, they bring energy and resilience to the job. Instead of feeling cynical and distant from their organizations, they feel deeply involved. Instead of feeling ineffective in their roles, they take pride in strong performance. These individuals are *engaged* with their work—a welcome state for both employees and managers that defines the opposite of burnout.

But there are other patterns, too. Sometimes a person frequently experiences a negative crisis, but only on one of these three dimensions, while the other two are relatively unproblematic or even positive. For example, a person might be exhausted on many occasions but still feel involved in their context and satisfied with their performance. Another person might have nagging feelings of ineffectiveness, making them chronically low on the self-evaluation dimension, but still approach tasks energetically and feel connected to the organization. Still another might be cynical and hostile about their employment context, while scoring high on energy and sense of effectiveness. Whichever dimension is the problem, it may amount to a unique challenge that can be managed to maintain a productive and fulfilling work life. But it might instead represent a step on the path toward the more broadly negative problem of burnout.

In fact, the different combinations of "scores" along these core dimensions make for myriad variations in experience and degrees of burnout and engagement. But the five possibilities just discussed— burnout, engagement, and the three conditions of acute problems along a single dimension—represent five useful "profiles." Defining these has provided a framework for our most recent research into the patterns of experience people have at work.[11] Here we encapsulate what these five highly distinct profiles look like and share how typical they are in workplaces.[12]

BURNOUT PROFILE

When someone experiences a high frequency of all three negative dimensions—exhaustion, cynical distancing, and low efficacy—that individual is encountering burnout. The occurrence and etiology of burnout begins with exhaustion, which often starts the domino effect. Cynicism takes the experience of exhaustion to another level, and in turn is compounded by inefficacy. Work, instead of bringing great satisfaction, fulfillment, and confirmation of one's identity, becomes a joyless burden to be minimized, avoided, and escaped. Basically, workers who are experiencing burnout are overwhelmed, unable to cope, and unmotivated, and they display negative attitudes and poor performance. The burnout profile is associated with serious mismatches in all six areas of job-person fit: workload, control, rewards, community, fairness, and values.

Past research studies have found that 10 to 15 percent of people in their occupational samples were experiencing the burnout pattern. This proportion has grown, however, during highly stressful times, such as among healthcare workers during the Covid-19 pandemic.

ENGAGEMENT PROFILE

The opposite profile from burnout, in which all three dimensions are frequently positive, is that of engagement. People who are engaged with their work have the energy to do the job, are deeply involved in their work tasks, and feel effective and successful in their accomplishments. They are ready to commit time and effort to their job, rather than feeling too tired and overwhelmed to do the work. They find their job activities to be meaningful, which heightens their involvement and motivation to do their work well. And when they succeed in accomplishing their tasks, they feel competent and effective. As expected, they show good job-person matches in all six areas of job-person fit.

Our observations have been that the engagement profile represents a more normative experience in the workplace. For the most part, things are going well for employees, and if occasional problems arise, these are likely to be temporary. Problems are more easily resolved if employees maintain good relationships with their work. At the beginning of a job experience, a person is likely to fit this profile, perhaps feeling hope that it will provide a steady income and some security, even if the work is not all that thrilling. Most people do not begin a job feeling burned out. But if there begins to be an erosion of their initial engagement—of their energy, involvement, and efficacy—that erosion can continue to eventual burnout.

We should note that *engagement* has turned out to be a popular term—and has been used by others to describe positive responses to work life. Despite the similar goal, these other definitions have differed, leading to a lack of clarity and some confusion about exactly what engagement means. Sometimes it has been used to describe a more intense peak experience, such as "bursting with energy."[13] Other times it has been used to mean that employees are so enthusiastic about their job that they go above and beyond to put in "discretionary effort."[14]

Interestingly, the engagement profile as we have defined describes about a third of the workforce—nearly equivalent to the percentages commonly reported by other measures of engagement (such as the Gallup Employee Engagement Index). This makes this profile about twice as prevalent as the burnout profile. Clearly, burnout is not the "majority experience," as is sometimes claimed.

OVEREXTENDED PROFILE

As we just saw, people in the burnout and engagement profiles together make up just about half of employees who have reported their experience. The other half can be clustered into the three remaining basic profiles based on which of the three core dimensions their most negative scores skew toward. The first of these is the overextended profile.

People who fit into this profile report that they are experiencing frequent exhaustion—but on other dimensions, their experience is not as negative. The major mismatch they are facing in the workplace is a very heavy workload, usually with high demands and long hours. They may believe in themselves and their work, but they are always worn out.

It should be noted that, just as *engagement* has been defined in several different ways, so too has *burnout*. As a result, the overextended profile is often misidentified as burnout—on the mistaken assumption that exhaustion is all there is to the burnout experience. It is not. The current work life crisis is not simply that people get tired a lot, but that their experience is negative along two other dimensions, as well. Focused solely on the individual effort dimension, and the negative experience of being overextended, this profile tends to characterize about 15 to 20 percent of the workforce at any one time.

DISENGAGED PROFILE

People in the disengaged profile, by contrast, may not be feeling exhausted. They might also feel they are doing a good job. But they are consistently cynical about their jobs and have lost the motivation that originally attracted them to their line of work. Although they do not have a mismatch with workload, they experience major difficulties in almost all other aspects of their job experience, including lack of control, insufficient rewards, and poor-quality social relationships. In some cases, they report being constrained from doing the right thing in their jobs, suggesting feelings of moral injury and compassion fatigue.

The powerful toxicity of cynicism makes this profile (as opposed to the overextended profile just discussed) the closest profile to full-blown burnout. It tends to be expressed by about 20 percent of the workforce.

INEFFECTIVE PROFILE

The main problem for people in the ineffective profile is a negative sense of their own professional accomplishments on the job. They may have energy, and they may care about the social context of the job, but perhaps the work is not intrinsically rewarding or they do not see themselves making any progress. Even if they contribute real effort, the results may seem trivial, and they may lose confidence in their ability to make a difference. The overall pattern of job-person fit is generally average or so-so: no serious mismatches, but also no strong positive matches.

This particular profile has been relatively understudied, largely because this third dimension—self-evaluation of efficacy—is often neglected and not assessed.[15] The ineffective profile, however, appears to be closer to the engagement profile than the others are, so it would be worthwhile to better understand what the problems are here and how they could be improved. There may be particular potential here to make work a more positive experience for people. This profile tends to characterize about 15 to 20 percent of the workforce at any one time.

The figure below shows the average scores on the areas of work life in each of the five profiles for a population of 2,300 healthcare providers.[16] The graph depicts important points about the model. On this graph, the midline represents the average scores for the areas of work life. Bars above the midline indicate a match: the

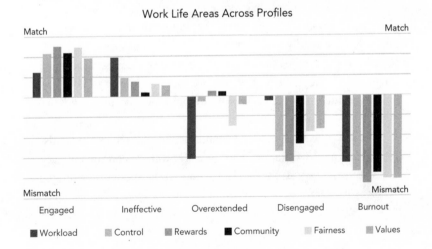

Work Life Areas Across Profiles

longer the bar, the more positive the match. Bars below the mid-line indicate a mismatch: the longer the bar, the more negative the mismatch.

For the engaged profile, all six areas are substantially positive. In contrast, for burnout, all six area are substantially negative. For the ineffective profile, all six areas are close to average. That profile does not indicate distress, nor does it indicate excitement about work. Everything is just average.

The overextended profile has a few mismatches, the largest of which is with workload. They have too much to do and lack the resources to meet those demands. The mismatch on fairness may be linked to their concern about workplace policies. In contrast, community is actually in the average range, while values is only a small distance into the mismatch range. These qualities suggest how those in the overextended profile maintain moderate or low levels of cynicism or inefficacy: they continue to connect with the people and the values of their workplaces. They are exhausted while working at an unsustainable pace, but they believe in what they're doing and see value in their contributions.

The disengaged profile experiences work life quite differently. Workload is not a big problem. The other five areas of work life, however, are solidly in the mismatch range. This pattern is consistent with the profile's low or moderate level of exhaustion, despite high levels of cynicism. They do not feel overwhelmed and may have confidence in their own efficacy, but they have no confidence in their workplace.

The severity of the burnout profile is reflected in its serious mismatches on all six areas of work life. They are overwhelmed, lack confidence in themselves, and have misgivings about everything in their workplace.

It's the Canary *and* the Coal Mine

The number one question we are always asked is this one: What can a person do about burnout? The underlying assumption lurking in that question is that burnout is only an individual problem. What follows from this is another assumption—that individuals who are experiencing burnout should be able to fix the problem by themselves.

There is nothing wrong with someone's taking personal steps to cope with chronic job stressors—indeed, it is something to be encouraged. What *is* wrong is assuming that such personal actions are sufficient to "fix" burnout and keep it from becoming a problem again. As we have seen, there are many good strategies that promote coping with job stressors, but that is different from *preventing* the stressors from occurring in the first place. Helping people to cope effectively with job stressors is certainly a positive thing to do—but it does not change the stressors themselves.

Remember that popular saying we mentioned earlier, about people working in adverse conditions: "If you can't take the heat, then get out of the kitchen." It is helpful to help people cope by figuring out how to adapt to the heat. But why not also figure out how to turn down the heat to a more reasonable temperature? Or provide better ventilation, or a more spacious kitchen design, or other changes that would make the kitchen conditions less onerous and more accommodating to all the people who work there? Coping strategies are good, but they are not enough; we also need to focus on prevention strategies if we want to truly lower the risk of burnout. And that means changing the way we think about people in the workplace.

Too often, the situational context is considered to be a "given." It is accepted as being right or normal or just fine—"it is what it is." The corollary to that proposition is that the person must adapt to whatever the situation is. All questions, and potential answers, are then limited to what to do about the individual person and how to help or change that person. This framework does not allow for, or encourage, questions and potential answers about what to do about the job—the situation in which the person lives and functions.

Focusing on the person is not enough. As the next chapter will show, we need to understand and work with the relationship between the person and the job, and to then develop strategies to find better matches between them.

3

Rethinking the Relationship between Person and Job

Where major advances in workplace well-being occur, they come through better workplace design, not through supplying organizations with tougher employees. When the canary begins to fade in the coal mine, the response is not to toughen up the bird, trying to make it more like a buzzard. It is to address the issues in the coal mine. In other work environments, too, we need to focus on the situations in which people work and make sure that surrounding job conditions support them in doing their jobs well.

We believe burnout is the result of a mismatch between employee and workplace. This understanding of the problem points to different solutions than the common, everyday advice to "increase your resilience"—which implies becoming more like the buzzard. A contrary view worth considering is that work is *not* fine. For many people, it places extraordinary demands on their time, energy, abilities, and emotional capacity. For many, it fails to fulfill their aspirations to do meaningful work, to be treated with respect, and to have their contributions genuinely recognized. Accordingly, having offered some ideas for the individual in Chapter 2, our focus now shifts to improving the relationship between the person and the job. When conditions are pushing people toward full burnout syndrome, the answer is not more resilience. A dysfunctional workplace is not something for people to endure. It is something to change.

Job-Person Match

Burnout is best conceptualized as a relationship problem—an issue with the fit, or match, between the person and the job. When there is a good match, the worker is likely to be engaged with the job and happy, energetic, confident, and ready to commit to a productive long-term relationship. But when there is a mismatch, the employee is more likely unhappy, exhausted, and cynical. A person in this situation may be unwilling to do more than the bare minimum, and ready to quit the relationship and leave for another job. In short, a worker experiencing a major mismatch is likely to experience burnout.

We should note that the basic concept of a job-person fit is not something new. It has been discussed since more than a century ago, when the rise of industrial engineering first focused managers on redesigning jobs for greater efficiency and selecting workers to fulfill the requirements of specific jobs. Those industrial engineering–minded managers essentially had two choices of how to achieve a good match, and the same two choices exist today: either fit the person to the job, or fit the job to the person.

The first approach, fitting the person to the job, starts from the position that the job in question has certain requirements—things to be done, and certain ways to do them—and then considers how a person should acquire and demonstrate the necessary knowledge, skills, and abilities to meet those. The main mechanism for bringing the person into alignment with the job is training in the specialized tasks it involves and the tools used to perform them. Yet jobs are not wholly defined by tasks—every job also has many other requirements, such as hours of work and people with whom the job-holder must interact—so there can be more to fitting people to jobs than just changing their skill sets. Helping people cope with other challenges of jobs represents a secondary strategy. Either way, however, whether training or coping is involved, the job is the "given" and the worker must be modified to fit it.

The second approach goes in the opposite direction, starting from the position that people require certain conditions to perform at their best and then asking how jobs can be reshaped to fit their needs. This means first considering human strengths and limitations, and then designing the job to work with the former and recognize the latter. We see this approach most explicitly in the work of ergonomics specialists and "human factors" engineers, whose solutions begin with considerations of people's physical and cognitive features. For example, if a person's body is put under strain by the posture or motions required to perform a repetitive task, this can lead to a musculoskeletal disorder such as tension neck syndrome, a ruptured or herniated disc, tendonitis, or carpal tunnel syndrome. Such disorders are the biggest category of workplace injuries (and thus of workers' compensation costs)—but they are preventable. Redesigning physical industrial and office equipment (such as chairs and workstations) so that the body is supported, rather than strained, produces a better job-person fit and reduces the risk of injury.

Likewise, with a better understanding of how people perceive and act on information (for example, how they notice warning signals and take corrective actions), engineers can redesign the information-processing equipment workers use. A prominent example of this is the redesign of airline cockpit displays to support better decision-making and reduce errors by pilots.

As established as the concept of job-person fit is, however, these examples point to a blind spot that existed for decades. Whether the approach was to fit the person to the job or the job to the person, the person was viewed as a set of physical or cognitive attributes. For a long time, that left a third and very important category of attributes out of the picture.

PSYCHOLOGICAL FIT

Recently, there has been a recognition that people's *psychological* attributes, such as their motives and emotions, are also important factors in job-person matches and mismatches. In fact, this was noted by the pioneer of Total Quality Management, W. Edwards Deming. Warning against narrowly conceived reward systems in organizations, he wrote, "We must preserve the power of intrinsic motivation, dignity, cooperation, curiosity, joy in learning, that people are born with."[1]

There is ample research showing that job stressors have negative impacts on psychological well-being, as well as on physical health. Studies have provided data on how people's emotional responses and self-concepts affect how they cope with such stressors. Currently, the evidence points to the importance of certain fundamental psychological needs and desired emotional states, and how the satisfaction of these is tied to improved personal and job outcomes. To be clear, these deep needs are not specific to people's relationships with their work; pursuit of them drives behaviors in all kinds of life settings, including home and the larger community. With the focus here, however, on the problem of burnout, these needs are highly significant to thinking about how to achieve a good match between the worker and the workplace.[2] Self-determination theory has identified that every person has key needs for autonomy, belongingness, and competence.[3] *Autonomy* refers to feeling ownership of one's own behavior and being able to act with a sense of volition and choice. Other words, such as personal control or independence, are also used to describe this need. In a work setting it is achieved when people feel they have appropriate say or discretion about how they carry out their job tasks. *Belongingness* refers to the basic human desire to achieve close relationships with other people and a sense of connection with them. Whether called by this name or using other terms such as affiliation or recognition, the need is for access to a positive and supportive social community. *Competence* refers to the desire to feel capable of meeting challenges, producing good outcomes, and learning things. One wants to be effective in accomplishing tasks and achieving goals. Together, the needs for autonomy, belongingness, and competence motivate people's behavior as they seek to grow and gain fulfillment.

Beyond these three fundamental pursuits that drive people's choices, there are four other significant psychological factors highly relevant to job-person match: these are the degrees to which people experience psychological safety, fairness, meaning, and positive emotions. *Psychological safety* refers to one's desire to be free of anxieties in contexts that may pose various social risks, such as being bullied, humiliated, or marginalized. Supporting this need in organizations may involve management policies and practices to protect people from harmful dynamics that would undermine trust and teamwork. *Fairness* refers to one's desire to be treated with respect and to know that any external decisions that affect one's life are unbiased and nondiscriminatory. At a group level, this can be discussed in terms of social justice. *Meaning* refers to one's desire to do things of value, which give purpose to one's life. Related terms here include personal growth and self-actualization, which focus more on achieving one's potential. Finally, by *positive emotions* we refer broadly to a range of pleasant feelings one wants to experience in life. A related concept is the notion of psychological capital, which sees positive emotions—especially hope, efficacy, resilience, and optimism—as a store of vital resources a person draws on and invests to accomplish things. Positive emotions have been linked to well-being and positive outcomes in organizations and are clearly part of a good match between worker and workplace.

All of these terms represent priorities for individuals in all spheres of their lives. In workplaces where people don't feel thwarted in their pursuits of autonomy, belongingness, and competence, and where they don't experience a lack of psychological safety, fairness, meaning, and positive emotions, their job performance and productivity is enhanced, along with their psychological well-being. Given the central importance of these factors to a person's experience of a job, they all represent good candidate targets for well-designed interventions to improve the job-person match.

How a Person-Only Focus Undermines Problem-Solving

When things are not going well in a workplace, there tends to be a lot of finger-pointing and blaming of specific other people or groups. Put-downs such as "the workers don't have what it takes" or "the bosses don't know what they are doing" are all too common. While it may be easier to cast blame or responsibility on individuals, this limits what questions are asked and what answers are given. This person-only point of view is typically adopted regarding burnout, and also regarding its opposite, work engagement, which is often perceived solely as an individual inclination toward enthusiasm or commitment or especially "discretionary effort"—the observable choice of an employee to go above and beyond what a job formally requires.

This tendency to focus on the person rather than the situation turns out to be a basic feature of human perception and understanding. It has often been described in terms of *figure and ground*—meaning that a person's attention naturally focuses on a main object of interest, or figure, while relegating other parts of the scene to the background, or ground. For example, a statue in a museum gallery may be the figure, and the wall hung with art behind it may be the ground. The page you are reading is the figure, and the setting you are peripherally aware of beyond it is the ground. When a person catches our interest, we perceive that individual as the figure and the surrounding situation as the ground. Moreover, the way we *think* about the person and the situation often reflects this figure-ground distinction.

Specifically, when we train our focus on a person as figure, rather than taking in the broader scene, we tend to make different causal attributions. Something has happened, in other words, and the mind is engaged in figuring out why it happened. If we have been focusing on a person as figure, our thinking is guided toward dispositional attributions—that is, seeing the event as the result of the individual's own behavior, as driven by that person's personality, intention, ability, intelligence, or other personal attributes. By contrast, bringing what was the "ground" into focus, thinking about the contextual elements that may constrain or trigger the individual's behavior, leads to situational attributions. In this case we are inclined, perhaps, to blame the rainy weather and wet pavement for the person's slip and fall, or the noisy children in the store for the clerk's rudeness. The cause of the occurrence is located outside the individual's person. Because humans have the tendency to focus on figures versus ground, and to cast other humans as figures, there is an inherent tendency to make more dispositional judgments than situational ones. This deeply ingrained cognitive bias has been called the *fundamental attribution error*.[4]

This error is common in workplaces. When there are problems, much more attention is focused on workers (as figures) and what is wrong with them than on the conditions of their jobs (the ground). In the case of burnout, this takes the form of people's assuming, if a worker is experiencing burnout, that the cause can be found within that person. Perhaps there is something fundamentally wrong with the individual. The job is what it is, and the worker has the responsibility to adjust to its constraints and adhere to its rules. In short, a dispositional explanation puts the burden on the worker to achieve a better fit or match with the job.

Broadening the focus to include an emphasis on the job situation in which a person operates provides a better basis for understanding all the worker profiles outlined in Chapter 2—and for addressing the distressed ones defined there as the burnout, disengaged, overextended, and ineffective profiles. The factors that disrupt people's relationships with their work are often situated in their work environments. Indeed, several contextual themes underlie virtually all descriptions of a distressed work experience. One ever-present theme is *imbalance*, often between high demands and low or inadequate resources. Another is the *chronic nature* of job demands or stressors; unlike occasional crises, they are present on an ongoing basis. Another theme concerns *conflict*—whether between people on the job (clients, colleagues, or managers), or between the demands of various roles an individual plays, or between important values in some degree of tension.

Shifting focus from the individual to the situation can also bring to light other contextual factors that can disrupt a person's relationship with the job. Most notably, these have to do with the person's "nonwork life"—the realms of home, family and friends, leisure activities, second jobs, and more. A default to dispositional attributions puts the burden on people to figure out how to resolve any conflicts they may have with the standard demands of their jobs, but a situational viewpoint could point to other solutions, such as flexible work hours.

THREE ESSENTIAL SHIFTS FROM PERSON-ONLY

If the hope is to go beyond coping strategies to preventive ones, then the way people have been considering the problem of burnout—the person-only framework we have been describing—must change in three important ways. First, it needs to shift from focusing on what may be wrong with the person and focus instead on what may be wrong in the relationship between the person and the *situation*.

Whether at work or at home or in the community, the individual is always thinking and acting within a larger context.

This focus on the situation is especially important when considering demographic factors, such as a person's sex or ethnicity or age. Too often, if a question about the importance of such a factor is raised—for example, *Is burnout more of a problem for men or for women?*—people look for an answer in terms of differences *within* people. If the men in a population show less incidence, for example, people might conclude it's "because men are stronger and tougher." If the women prove more resistant to burnout, they might say that is "because women are more nurturant and sociable." Both explanations ignore situational circumstances that may do much more to distinguish men's and women's experiences. For example, if the great majority of certain especially burnout-prone roles in an organization are filled by men, or by women, then sex and job are confounded, and these variables cannot be easily untangled. But even when men and women occupying the same job exhibit different patterns of burnout, it can still be true that situational factors are making their experiences different. In an early study of public service workers, for example, we found a clear pattern among holders of the same service representative job. The women were more satisfied than the men.[5] When we dug into why this was so, however, it turned out that the larger career path in which this job was situated was different for the women than the men. Most of the women, who lacked college degrees, experienced being promoted to the service representative position as a desirable, upward move that brought more prestige, better pay, and more job security than they had had before. Most of the men were in a different situation: they held college degrees and had accepted the service representative job only as an entry-level position from which they hoped to soon move on.

To look at the larger situational context of a job is to consider all the roles, groups, rules, and systems that shape the behavior of the people who work in that job. As an example, when we interviewed staff in one public service organization where burnout was a concern, we heard regular complaints about how supervisors responded to their efforts. As one person described it, "I never get positive feedback, no matter how well I do the job—it's always, 'Nice job, but . . .' and then some negative criticism. It can be demoralizing! I always hope that someday I will just hear 'Nice job.' Period. Just that, with no 'but' after it." Later, however, when we interviewed the supervisors themselves, we learned that they had all been trained to give feedback in just that way: the model was to say something positive first, then follow it with a "negative" that could be improved. From their perspective they were adhering to what they were taught and doing their jobs well, and it was shocking to learn that the people reporting to them were unhappy and frustrated by the interactions.

All kinds of situational constraints on an individual worker's behavior can raise or lower the potential of burnout, and these come into sharper focus when the emphasis is not on the person only, but on the relationship between the person and the job context. When, for example, are they supposed to arrive and leave a formal workplace? What tasks are they supposed to do? How must they do them, and by when? How are they expected to consult and communicate with others? Who has authority over whom? Are any deviations from or exceptions to the rules allowed in unusual circumstances? Who can make independent decisions of what kinds?

At the outset of this section we stated that three shifts are required to the person-only framework that people usually bring to burnout problems—and we have just argued for the biggest shift. The framework needs to shift from what may be wrong *with the person* to focus instead on what may be wrong *in the relationship between the person and the situation.* To introduce the second required shift, we should note the potential danger with the first. It would be a problem if, by framing burnout as a paired construction, we caused thinking about it to devolve into oppositional, "either-or" terms. If there is a mismatch, that is, which side of the equation is to blame? This kind of thinking still leads to a lot of finger-pointing, so another adjustment to the framework will be helpful in the search for viable solutions.

The second needed shift is to frame burnout in "both-and" terms. That is, *both* the individual *and* the context play roles in causing it and relieving it. It is the relationship between individual and context that is critical here, key to understanding burnout and figuring out what to do about it. What is causing people to be in sync with their jobs, or experiencing major disconnects? Which areas are likely to be the "trouble spots," and which are likely to be sources of success and comfort? With the goal being to forge a good fit, or match, a focus on the relationship between the person and the job has the advantage of moving analysis beyond "either-or" finger-pointing to highlighting more of what is taking place within the job environment.

Finally, a third shift required to get to a good match is to focus more on what could be right, rather than simply on what is wrong. What might be a better way to assign job tasks, or to provide constructive feedback, or to improve team discussions? And once a good option has been identified, how can it be implemented successfully? There is a general tendency to focus on the negative—every hassle, every action that fails or goes wrong, every obstacle—and to complain about these and look for someone to blame. It may be easier to point out what's wrong (and moan and groan about it) than it is to point out what would be right—but working to generate positive solutions is essential if things are going to be changed for the better.

Essential Steps toward Good Matches

Across the years, as we have spoken with different occupational groups about burnout, we have routinely included a presentation about the six different areas that can be drivers of burnout. These are the mismatches we already previewed in Chapter 1: work over-load, lack of control, insufficient rewards, breakdown of community, absence of fairness, and values conflicts. One recurring presenta-tion we have done is an annual one with a group of PhD students in the physical sciences who have organized support groups to help them cope with the stresses of their laboratory training jobs. One time, a woman who had attended the talk a few years earlier came back and shared this story with us:

> As I was growing up, I always knew I wanted to pursue a career in science, so when I was accepted into the graduate program and assigned to a prestigious lab, I was in heaven! But the lab turned out to be a hellish experience for me—it was difficult to deal with the other lab students, the supervisors, and the professor in charge. I was not successful in my work, and I couldn't turn things around. So I was facing a crisis moment of "maybe I am not actually good enough to work in this field." I was thinking that I would have to quit the program and give up my dream, because I was a failure and not cut out for this kind of career.
>
> And then I attended your talk four years ago and heard about the six areas—and I was going down the list, saying, "Check, I have work overload ... check, it's a socially toxic community ... yes, check unfairness, too"—and suddenly I realized that *all six* of them were big mismatches for me. And then I had that light bulb moment: "It's not that I'm not good enough—I am in the wrong lab!"
>
> So, I worked with an adviser to get out of the lab I was in and switch to another lab—not an easy thing to do, but I persisted—and eventually I got a new position in this other lab. And that lab job turned out to be a great match for me. I have been able to do good work, and I have become a coau-thor on some scientific articles, and now I am out on the job

market and have already gotten invited for some job interviews! Understanding what was going on in the six areas really changed my perspective on what was going wrong—and it wasn't just about me.

In the same way, many people find it helpful to use the six dimensions of job-person match to assess their employment situations. Doing so clarifies what is and is not working well in their own circumstances. In this woman's case, the conclusion was that there was so much wrong with the match that her best option was to leave her job and seek a better alternative. But often, the problems employees face are not so pervasive, and it is possible to identify changes that could be made within specific areas to improve the job context and make the workplace one in which they can thrive.

Recall that part of the World Health Organization's statement on burnout, quoted in the introduction, is that it results "from chronic workplace stress that has not been successfully managed." From that management perspective, making progress is a matter of taking a set of basic steps. As we will explain more fully below, the first is to zero in on a target area, based on a positive orientation to achieving a better match, and the subsequent steps are to set an attainable goal, redesign to achieve a better match, outline a plan to make the change happen, and make use of effective practices. All of these steps should be approached collaboratively, with a bias toward customized approaches, and with unwavering commitment to building engagement.

PIVOT TO CONSIDER POSITIVE MATCHES

The first essential step toward a better job-person match is to focus on an area where there is clear potential for improvement—knowing that there are many types of chronic stressors that could be better managed, and therefore many choices that could be made. To make the right choice, the fundamental first move should be to pivot to a positive orientation. Each of the six areas of mismatch we presented in Chapter 1 can be seen as the worst case in a wide range of possibilities, and each has its opposite at the positive end of the spectrum. An ideal job-person match, therefore, would feature these six positive conditions:

- Sustainable workload

- Ample choice and control

- Gratifying recognition and rewards

- Supportive work community

- Norms of fairness, respect, and social justice

- Well-aligned values and meaningful work

By focusing on the positive endpoints, it is possible to find the targets with biggest potential to improve job-person matches. Meanwhile, dividing the opportunity into six lines of consideration offers other benefits. It means that many possible reasons for the problem will surface and many possible options for improvement will be generated. It helps to head off any temptation to seek a standard, universal recipe; looking at the opportunity from different angles makes it clearer that every organization and group of workers represents a unique mix of these six areas and calls for a tailored solution. It also facilitates collaborative thinking about solutions to focus on these areas specifically. For example, if the focus is not broadly on burnout or engagement but more narrowly on workload, people can trade ideas with greater shared clarity: "What if we change our workflow in this certain way, to even out the cycles of intense effort and downtime? Could that get us to a more sustainable workload?" Or, if the discussion is centered on recognition and rewards: "The all-staff picnic has been a traditional way the company expresses appreciation for everyone's contributions. What would be some other ways to do that?"

Perhaps most valuable of all, starting the search for targets by assessing all six areas provokes thinking in unaccustomed ways about problems and solutions. These multiple perspectives help "break set"—that is, allow people to break away from set patterns of thinking to question their implicit assumptions, ingrained operating procedures, and "same old, same old" practices that have not worked. For example, in one case we will discuss in Chapter 8, a CEO first assumed that, to the extent that employees were burned out, it must be a problem of workload or rewards. It turned out to be one of *fairness*. Even after that discovery challenged his instincts, he stuck to a further assumption that perceptions of unfairness could be fixed by more money. They could not—because the problem was not about uneven rewards, it was about arbitrary practices.

With a positive orientation toward change and any of the six desired matches in focus, there are many ways to generate alternative ideas for achieving the goal. Our recommendation is to recognize the role of the core psychological needs just discussed in people's well-being and work motivation, and use these as guides for redesigning job tasks and organizational processes in ways that will provide better job-person matches.

So how do we do this? Having articulated these deep psychological needs, how do we figure out practical ways to satisfy one or more of them on the job? At first glance, the task may not seem as intuitive as figuring out how to meet physical needs—for example, by redesigning a chair that provides greater support and comfort. The two are more similar, however, than one might think. The trick is to get information from people about the conditions that satisfy a particular need. For example, just as they might tell you they felt most comfortable in a chair they could adjust to their height and workstation setup, they can tell you that their most satisfying level of autonomy in a job was when they exercised a certain level of discretion regarding how they went about doing what they needed to accomplish.

A useful procedure for gaining these insights is the *critical incident technique*.[6] In formal social science research, this long-established method gathers input from study participants by asking them to recall and tell about a time they experienced the phenomenon in question. What happened, and what was the outcome? Applied to job-person matches and mismatches, this can take the form of asking employees to consider a certain core psychological need and to share an anecdotal account of a time when it was especially supported (or thwarted) in their work experience. For instance: "Please describe a specific work situation where you felt you were treated with great *fairness*." Replies are guided to include the background and setting of the story (where it happened, who was present, what was the situation); the behaviors that occurred in the situation (the teller's own behaviors, others' behaviors, organizational or environmental events); the immediate outcomes of those behaviors or changes (the direct responses made by the employee and others, and how they represented a change in perception or cognition); and the longer-term consequences or personal outcomes caused by the incident (for both the organization and the employee, perhaps as it altered their subsequent decision-making).

What is important to note here is that, while information is being gathered from individuals, the objective is to aggregate what is learned to identify shared job solutions, not just to know individual preferences. Once multiple critical incidents have been collected from a group of employees (perhaps a team, unit, or cohort holding the same job title) these accounts can be combined into an overall picture of key themes of need satisfaction and workplace characteristics associated with those needs. The results can then be shared with the employees in a next phase of asking them to generate ideas about improvements that might increase the frequency of such positive experiences of need satisfaction on the job.

It is important that the individuals sharing critical incidents or otherwise reporting their own experiences know that the information they provide is not being used to diagnose or fix their particular cases, but rather to help shape job modifications for the benefit of many workers. It would be unfortunate if a one-on-one interview technique reinforced the impression that burnout is a problem of the individual and left people asking, "What can I do about it?" The process of addressing burnout, and working toward better job-person matches, should feel like a "we" effort, not a "me" one.

SET ATTAINABLE GOALS

With the focus trained on an area with high potential for positive change, and ideas for improvement already generated, the challenge arises of how to choose which ideas to pursue and in what order. As in other realms, the vision of the future must be translated into an initial change strategy. It matters how you start.

One important criterion is, of course, that the first change should be something meaningful—in an area people really care about. At the same time, it should represent a "doable" change, with good prospects for successful implementation in the near term. It is always a challenge to change something that has become established in an organization. It takes time and effort and there are glitches and course corrections along the way. But it is especially important for people to see the first steps of a long-term initiative working out successfully. Early victories are cause for celebration, provide motivation to take on more challenging changes, and build hope for a better future.

An attainable goal typically implies small changes rather than big ones. By "small" we do not mean trivial or silly or inconsequential. Any stressor that persistently irritates workers is certainly a candidate for a meaningful fix, and if that fix is within reach, it may well rise to the top of the to-do list. A minor stressor can act like a pebble in one's shoe. The pain and frustration it causes may be low-level, but it is constant—and it's a great relief when it is lessened or eliminated. If employees could choose the top five "pebbles" in their jobs, which ones would be on everyone's list?

Often, the temptation is to take aim first at other kinds of stressors: the big boulders compared to those small pebbles. Projects targeted at these not only engage with critical and highly meaningful issues but offer the potential for transformational effects. (An example is the values clarification process we will describe in Chapter 9.) But a boulder of a problem can also be so big and complex that it is hard to get one's arms around, and thus a project can be less sure to succeed or take much longer to yield results. Before tackling these very challenging areas, it may be wise to establish a viable process for making change by working on more attainable goals.

REDESIGN FOR A BETTER MATCH

Once a positive, attainable goal has been chosen, the change strategy needs to develop a good solution for achieving it. In some cases, that may entail a straightforward investment, such as in better equipment and supplies. If people want less of their time to be wasted by a nonworking printer, for example, the answer can be as simple as a newer machine and larger stock of paper. But often, another solution is possible, too. Maybe it becomes part of someone's role to keep the printer in good working order, or the process the whole team follows is changed to deliver more documents electronically. Later, in Chapter 10, we will discuss solution design more thoroughly, but a few key principles of redesign should be mentioned here, as part of any change strategy.

One principle is that the best solutions emerge from consideration of many solutions. The idea is to generate multiple potential solutions, and then assess the pros and cons of each of them. For every answer proposed to *What could we do?* there should be multiple follow-on questions: Why would that be better than other alternatives? What are the costs or trade-offs? How does this actually improve the fit on this area, in terms of control, community, fairness, and more?

Another principle is that effective solutions serve key psychological needs. Part of the consideration of alternative change ideas should be an explicit effort to identify what key psychological needs might be involved, and how these could inform any redesigns. For example, a solution might be suggested to resolve a problem of unfairness, such as favoritism. How does that solution connect to the need for psychological safety? Or there might be an idea for improving the social climate in a work community. It would serve people's need for belongingness, but could it do more by also responding to their need for meaning?

A third principle is the often neglected one of *subtraction*—if tasks and responsibilities are being added to a job, then some other things need to be taken away. What tasks are no longer necessary and can simply be deleted? Can some tasks be redesigned or reformatted to be done more easily and quickly, thus subtracting unnecessary time and effort? Or can a time-consuming task be shifted to someone else—and if so, what can be taken off *their* plate? Many overloaded jobs are the result of steady accretion over the years—things keep getting added to the work people are already doing, and rarely does anything get removed. Even more rare is a substantial review of organizational procedures and redesign of processes (a sort of major spring cleaning). Occasionally, managers should step back and reassess: "Given how we operate now, with our resources and technology, how could we design a better workflow for the important things we do?"

MAKE THE CHANGE HAPPEN

To bring about a desired change, it is not enough to simply announce that "from now on, we're going to do things this way." It has to be a collective enterprise, with everyone on board and willing to give up something familiar (even if it is disliked) for something new and hopefully better. The implementation process needs to be well planned, and it needs to specify milestones of progress. What will it take to make this work, and how will we know that we remain on track? In the end, what will success look like?

Again, meaningful change does not happen overnight. A realistic plan factors in the time it will take to shed old ways of doing things and learn new ones, to reach the point where they are automatic, to deal with unexpected bugs and hiccups, and to tweak things until they are right. It is important to keep regular progress reports on the agenda, to celebrate small wins and good revisions. And when the goal has been accomplished satisfactorily, celebrate that, too—and share it with others who could benefit from it.

COLLABORATE, CUSTOMIZE, COMMIT

In Part III of this book, where the discussion moves to practical challenges in creating better job-person matches and making them work, we will delve further into key change practices that employers can employ. Because the success of any change, large or small, depends on employee buy-in and willingness to make it work, those driving changes in workplaces should keep in mind these three Cs: collaborate, customize, and commit.

By *collaborate*, we mean that managers in organizations should not act unilaterally on their own conclusions as to what would help. They should ask employees to be a part of making things better. Ask for ideas and feedback on various alternatives, and then listen to what people contribute. If employees do not see the potential benefit of a proposed change, it will not happen.

Also important is being willing and able to *customize*. This is particularly true of "best practices" observed to be working in other organizations. In reality, it is never true that one size fits all, and there must be thoughtful adaptation of proposed changes to each local culture and type of occupation. Encouraging creative modifications also helps a solution become more accepted, because it is "ours."

Organizations must also be prepared to *commit*. Achieving positive improvements will require sustained effort, with cycles of making positive interventions, evaluating their results, and proceeding with further modifications. Work toward creating better job-person matches may not succeed at first, but it is important that the people of the organization keep on trying until they get it right.

Why Matches Matter

The author of *The Happiness Track* recounts a youthful experience she had, working as an intern at an international newspaper in Paris, France. Her summer job had her frequently delivering messages and documents between two parts of the building: the floor where the writers and editors were preparing the written content for the next morning's edition, and the basement where the press workers would print it before dawn. Although both groups worked under the same daily deadline pressure, their two work environments were starkly different, not only in terms of the tasks to be done and the people doing them, but in the workplace climate. On the writers' floor the atmosphere was tense as people hunched anxiously over computer keyboards, eating at their desks and generally keeping to their cubicles. The printing room was noisy and festive, with people joking and laughing with each other, and a spread laid out on a table of French bread, cheese, and wine. Not surprisingly, the intern always felt better on entering the printing room, leading her later to write, "I believe most of us want to be like the French press workers: we want to do a good job—and we want to enjoy doing it."[7]

Doing a good job and feeling good about doing it—this is a great way of expressing the core goal of promoting a good job-person match. The six areas of mismatch matter because they resonate with the psychological needs and states identified in this chapter. A basic approach to improving the relationships of people with their workplaces starts with finding out which of these domains are working well for people, which are presenting problems, and to what degree those represent intractable problems in their quests for fulfillment.

As we move into the six chapters that make up Part II of this book, we pivot to the positive, examining actual settings in which organizations rethought problems, designed solutions, and allowed changes for the better to emerge. And as each chapter puts the spotlight on a different area—workload, control, reward, community, fairness, and values—the bigger message will become clear: there are many kinds of positive job-person matches that can be made, and many different paths to achieving them.

PART II

The Mismatches

4

Workload

The Japanese word *karoshi* means "death due to overwork," or more specifically, as it was defined in 1989 by the Council for Karoshi Victims, the "fatal condition in which the living rhythm of a human being is collapsed due to excessive fatigue and the life maintenance function is ruined."[1] The most common medical causes of karoshi are heart attacks and strokes due to long working hours, sleep deprivation, and exhaustion.

More recently, a distinction has been made between karoshi in general and the more specific case of *karo-jisatsu*, which means "suicide due to overwork." For karo-jisatsu, the causes go beyond physical stressors to include psychosocial ones, many of which are also risk factors for burnout and depression. Understanding karoshi clearly involves awareness of certain cultural factors. One of these is the value placed on "loyalty to the organization"—which in a broad sense sounds positive but is often assessed narrowly in terms of maximizing "desk time," never saying no to the boss, and never going home before the boss does. Loyalty also means that workers routinely cut short their vacations if called upon, or forego time off altogether. Another cultural factor is the expectation that employees will engage in "service overtime"—that is, unpaid activities such as entertaining customers in the evenings or on weekends. At first, it was only men who were at risk for karoshi—because the men in Japanese society were the sole breadwinners of their households while women stayed home and raised children. Now that more Japanese women are in the workforce, they are at risk for karoshi, too. In one case, when a thirty-one-year-old journalist died of heart failure, it was discovered she had worked 159 hours of overtime in her last month.[2]

Besides karoshi and karo-jisatsu, there are other names to describe (or even justify) doing more work and spending more time at work—the "always on" or "go, go, go" or "grind" or "hustle" culture. Among China's technology professionals, there is a "996" culture of working from nine in the morning till nine at night, six days a week (despite labor laws restricting the workday to eight hours). The hope is that more productivity will mean more money and more job security as the inevitable rewards of working longer and harder. Those wishes do not always come true, however. More inevitable are exhaustion and poor health.

In some occupations, it is common to hear people saying, "I'm working six days a week—nights, weekends, holidays!" The problem is especially pronounced in some sectors, such as high-tech and health care. More people today report that they frequently feel very tired or exhausted than was typical in surveys several decades ago.[3] Recently, the focus has been on the younger generations of workers, with members of the so-called Gen Y (or millennials) so exhausted and sleep-deprived that sleep experts have also nicknamed them the "tired generation."[4] And so, as we launch into a series of chapters devoted to the six domains of job-person match, workload is a good place to start.

There are other factors besides long hours and heavy workload that create the overwork environment, including financial stressors such as insufficient pay, student debt, or the need to take on a second job. But the workload problem itself is substantial. When we created the worker profiles outlined in Chapter 2, it was clear that the exhaustion of people in the burnout profile and overextended profile was primarily caused by work overload. Where there is also an attitude that nothing can be done to change it, workload brings with it the anxiety of lacking control. One analyst explained it to us this way:

> Burnout has not been attended to by upper-level management. Most of the commentary we have heard on the topic is "we hear your pain" and "be patient." Neither of these approaches are helpful. The latest advice (published in an article in our company newsletter) said little more than advising supervisors to "talk about expecting a larger workload" or "overwork happens." Sometimes just the thought of how one's workload will increase (when someone else is leaving or a major system is changing) can cause anxiety. And if we are frequently asked to put in extra hours, we begin to question management's ability to plan appropriately, and we lose trust in their authority. If people feel overworked, it may be because they need a different mix of competencies on that project.

The job demands are too many, the hours are too long, and the resources to handle them are too few. Where workload is a major mismatch leading to burnout, there are three essential ways to improve the situation, and this chapter will explore them in turn. The first is to focus on *recovery* from working long and hard, rebuilding strength and enhancing resiliency to safeguard people's physical and mental well-being. The second is to achieve better *balance* between resources and demands, whether by increasing the former or reducing the latter. And the third is to set clear *boundaries* between work and nonwork—an area of growing challenges, where new solutions must be found to protect people's personal home lives.

Recovery

A basic truth about human beings is that, if they are to function when they are awake, they need sleep. This cycle of human renewal is at the core of our lifelong health and well-being. If we shortchange it, we pay the price in the short and long term. Therefore, working harder and harder in an unrelenting way is neither sustainable nor a way to succeed. To be most productive, one needs to balance periods of active, energetic, and high-intensity behavior with periods of rest and relaxation, when one's mind and body can recover and rebound.

The twenty-four-hour renewal cycle is usually conceptualized as the balance between wakefulness and sleep, and research has found that a third of that time (about seven to eight hours) is needed for a good, restorative rest. Unfortunately, many people fail to get the sleep they need—to the extent that sleep deprivation is now considered a public health issue in the United States. When people do not get enough sleep, they are more likely to be tired during the day and to have low energy, are more forgetful and less able to focus attention and concentrate on a task (and thus more likely to make errors), and are more prone to irritability, anxiety, and depression. Obviously, overwork can be a cause of sleep deprivation. Indeed, in the overwork culture, the macho "bragging rights" earned by deliberately going without sleep to complete a task—"I was up more than forty hours to get this thing done!"—are a characteristic feature.

Other disruptions can also interfere with sleep, however, and one of the major sources of such disruptions in our modern world is technology. More specifically, the disruption occurs when people are so fixated on their electronic devices, such as cell phones, that they do not truly disconnect when it is time to get ready for sleep. They are on the phone up to the moment they go to bed, it is glowing by their bed during the night (with not only periodic noises but also blue-spectrum light sending signals to pay attention rather than stay asleep), and it has the power to overwhelm them with information of all kinds, some of which is distressing enough to keep them lying awake. Members of younger generations, typically more adept with new technology devices and in the habit of using them every waking hour, may be at more risk for this kind of sleep disruption.

Technology must be managed—and managing it means balancing *on* and *off* time. People have to be able to "power down" to get the restful sleep they need, turning off and putting away devices that might interfere with that process of recovery and renewal. The transition to a good sleep can be helped if a person does something else to unwind, such as reading a book or magazine, taking a warm bath, or watching a comedy show—and can thus stop doing or thinking about work. Getting eight hours of good sleep should be treated as the basic necessity it is, rather than an option.

So, if eight hours per day should be devoted to restful sleep, what about the remaining time? How should the sixteen awake and active hours be divided across professional work life and personal home life?

An important response to that question was voiced more than a century and a half ago. In 1856, a group of stonemasons in Australia went on strike, demanding that their working hours be reduced. When the strike ended, the stonemasons had won the right to an eight-hour working day—a settlement that turned out to be historic, as it established the norm that a third of the day was the appropriate amount of time to be devoted to paid employment. Eight hours was subsequently enshrined in many labor laws around the world and is still the dominant rule (even if it gets ignored by overwork cultures like 996). This left the same amount of time for personal, "nonwork" activity. According to a workers' song from the 1800s, the ideal model was:

Eight hours to work,
Eight hours to play,
Eight hours to sleep,

Eight bob a day.
A fair day's work
For a fair day's pay.[5]

For many decades, the classic eight-hour span of work has been
"nine to five"—but in fact, whatever the formal shift, work-related
activity tends to chip away more of what could be play and sleep
time. Most obvious are the commuting demands that have become
such prominent parts of people's life rhythms, as they spend hours
of "nonwork" time in morning and evening traffic jams, just getting to and from work. Some people who work two (or even three)
jobs to pay their bills find it isn't possible to go back home between
shifts and end up napping in their cars in parking lots to make up
for missed sleep. Surveys across years reveal more work being
brought home, as people increasingly devote evening and weekend
hours to grading school papers and exams, filling out electronic
medical records, and answering business emails. In all of these ways,
work time expands at the expense of sleep and personal time, and
problems can arise as that imbalance not only prevents full rest and
recovery but affects social relationships and takes away from other
important life experiences.

What role should workplaces and management play in the recovery process? Most importantly, they should support the renewal
cycle. There should be sensible limits on work hours and a focus
on how employees will complete tasks within that time rather than
be forced to donate personal or sleep hours to finish their work.
There should also be clear support for work breaks, allowing employees to rest and recharge during their shifts. Some companies
have redesigned their physical work environments to include comfortable places for breaks away from desks or workstations, rooms
for short "power naps," and spaces for physical exercise, yoga, and
outdoor walks. To demonstrate an organization's commitment to

rest and recovery, it helps if managers themselves visibly make use of such resources. Also important is for them to encourage people to go home when their shifts are over, take their full breaks, and use up their vacation days.

One hospital leader described preventing overwork in the nursing team as a basic managerial responsibility: "If I find people continually staying ten hours instead of eight, then I talk to them about it. I remind them that we have three shifts for a very good reason, and I suggest they go home and let the next shift take over. This happens to head nurses and supervisors, too. When it does, we sit down and discuss what they're feeling, what they can do about it, what kind of help they need with their job. A lot of times, I tell them to take four days off and relax."[6]

Back to the topic of technology, it should be noted that, applied in the right ways, communications and information technology can be part of a person's recovery rather than disrupting it. As one worker who had suffered from burnout writes, "Ironically, the solution is probably to be found in the area which can also cause the problem: technology can help many employees work at times and places where they are most productive, and that may not be during conventional working hours or in an office setting." For that to work, however, she adds that "organizations need to build a culture of trust to underpin that flexibility" and focus on performance "in ways that are not about being physically present or 'always on.'"[7] Managers should think more creatively about how technology can allow workload parameters to be changed and reduce the impact of everyday stressors.

Balance on the Job

Although it may be possible to tolerate the occasional bout of overwork—perhaps staying up all night to finish a critical task and then recovering afterward—allowing that kind of imbalance to happen often is not compatible with staying healthy and happy and having a good life outside of the workplace. The impact does not stay behind in the workplace when the workers leave. It follows them wherever they go and often brings them down, both physically and socially, even when they are no longer on the job. In an insidious way, work can take over more and more of a person's life.

Sometimes workers try to resist a prevailing overwork culture. Recently, in China, some younger workers have rebelled against the 996 culture by slowing down and doing less. They make up an online community sharing and cheering on each other's tactics, from making more trips to the bathroom, to taking frequent breaks for stretches and refreshments in the work pantry, to posting on social media and playing video games. Some people would call this laziness, but the workers say they are reclaiming their right to work at a humane pace. Their name for it is "touching fish." That's a play on a Chinese proverb—*Muddy waters make it easy to catch fish*—which means that any time of turmoil presents opportunities to enrich oneself. In this case, the chaotic time has been the Covid-19 pandemic, when lockdowns pushed people into remote work arrangements and away from the watchful eyes of managers. Despite the mischievous tone, the movement has its roots in serious concerns about the recent rise in worker deaths. One software company has begun documenting companies that enforce excessive overtime in a project it calls 996.ICU—a shorthand warning that working 996 will land you in an intensive care unit.[8]

This kind of "slacker rebellion" can take hold where management and employees are not on the same page about workload, hours, and the need for breaks. Everyone needs opportunities to reboot—to rest, restore, and recharge—and these need to be recognized as normal parts of operating and built into the rhythm of the workday rather than viewed as drains on productivity. Some managers may persist in thinking their chief role is to police employees, but the best solutions for achieving better balance will come out of respectful collaboration with them. In a situation, for example, where some realignment of tasks and resources has to be made for a deadline to remain reasonable, it makes sense for a manager to pull team members into a discussion of how best to make adjustments. A team's manager can also take a more proactive stance to protect it from demands that are arbitrary, poorly thought-out, or too extreme. The mutual goal should always be to figure out the best work processes for getting the job done well by everyone, without social and personal collateral damage from poorly managed stressors.

What has become increasingly clear is that the best way to prevent burnout in *people* is to design organizational *processes* that enable them to do their work effectively. For example, surveys of physicians routinely find that their workdays are too crowded with bureaucratic tasks, their hours are too long, and they don't have enough control or autonomy to do their jobs well. (All this has long been true, predating the Covid-19 pandemic by many years.) What do physicians think would help reduce burnout? More manageable work schedules, more support staff, and more reasonable patient loads, among other things. And they are right, according to a recent review of strategies to alleviate physician burnout, which found that the most effective ones were organization-directed interventions, such as process changes, reductions of clerical burdens, and better team-based care.[9] "Most physicians are as efficient as possible, limited primarily by the inefficiencies of the systems in which they work," reports *Medscape*. "We should exhaust every other strategy for making the environment more sustainable—better tools, better processes, better workflows, better administrative support at every level—allowing doctors to work smarter instead of harder."[10]

The idea of "working smarter instead of harder" is an anti-burnout philosophy that has been touted for decades and needs to be implemented on a regular basis, especially for the small *changes* that are often not on anyone's radar screen. For example, one strategy for working smarter is to get rid of clutter—all the things that get in the way of getting the job done, that mess things up and waste people's time, that slow things down for no good reason, that cause confusion and even chaos, and that are really no longer necessary or required. How can we subtract some of these sources of clutter, so that the important job tasks are not weighed down by such unimportant untidiness? A reflexive response in many workplaces when a new problem or new need comes along is to make additions—a new form here, a new rule there—but not to match those with subtractions of what is now redundant, no longer needed, or irrelevant. To avoid overload, more should always be balanced with less, and this is as true at the individual level as at the organizational one. If another demand or opportunity is added to someone's plate, what is being removed to make room for it?

One lawyer noted that, in the past, she was reluctant to say no for fear of missing out on leadership opportunities: "I was afraid that if I did, everything might disappear." More recently, she has replaced that "scarcity" mentality with one that instead presumes abundance. "Now if I feel overextended, I'll ask myself: Is there a way to inject joy back into this role, or is it time to give it up? And I understand that when I want to take something on, I need to decide what to give up in order to make space."[11]

Most workers' jobs require a variety of tasks, some of which they find pleasant to do but others of which are more frustrating. When the latter start dominating the workday, a person might want to withdraw completely from the situation, such as by not coming to work. But in some workplaces, employees are able to periodically request a "work shift" for a day or more, moving them off the front lines of the work they find stressful and allowing them to devote hours to calmer tasks while others fill in for them temporarily. As an example, in one psychiatric ward, nurses having a rough week could arrange to step away from working directly with patients. "There are times on the ward when I know that I'm not as capable of giving that much of myself," explained one of them, "so I'll sit in the office and do a lot of paperwork. The way our schedule is, it gives you the opportunity to do that. You can withdraw and choose to attend meetings for a while. Or you can ask to get assigned to medications, so that you spend the entire day in the medicine room. Then, the only time you see patients is when you're calling on them for medicines." In this system, as one nurse shifts work, other nurses provide coverage so that patient care doesn't suffer.[12]

Note that this workplace system of shifting tasks among employees to achieve a better balance is dependent on two other areas of work-life: control and community. The system is a flexible one in which workers have some say about temporary adjustments to their schedule, and as we will see later in the next chapter, flexibility is an important part of a better job-person fit for control and autonomy. The system also depends upon good working relationships among the nurses on the team, which is a central element of a supportive workplace community. All nurses must play a part in the system and trust each other, so that everyone knows that they can ask for help with coverage when they need it, but that they must also provide that responsive help for their colleagues.

Boundaries between Work and Nonwork

The third eight-hour component of the human renewal cycle, after sleep and work, is "nonwork"—otherwise known as "personal" or "home" or "play." In truth, it is a combination of all three. This is the part of waking life when people are doing all kinds of nonwork things, ranging from spending time with different people (family, friends, neighbors) to doing errands or chores, to cooking, to participating in various activities (concerts, sports, religious services, school, the gym), to traveling for pleasure, and so on. For quite some time, the general assumption has been that this segment of personal life does not include any workplace tasks. Research on recuperation

and unwinding after work has shown that people work more productively and feel better when they can fully separate themselves
from their work for some of their day.[13] Deep recovery works best
when they can avoid giving any thought to their jobs, so drawing a
boundary line between work and nonwork has been vital to people's
health and personal growth.

As work has become more portable, however, boundaries have
become more permeable. The shift to "knowledge-based" econo-
mies in developed countries allows work to occur with less concern for time and place. Laptops, tablet computers, and mobile
phones have become the primary tools of the trade in many lines
of work. Clients have come to expect services and purchasing opportunities at any time they are awake. Many workplaces interact
with partners and clients globally, vastly expanding the definition
of "business hours." Nowadays, much work can be completed at
home, at a workshare site, in a coffee shop, or in transit. In some
cases, external locations work better for people than their office settings. Beyond the savings in commuting time and expense, other
settings may be more conducive to concentration, especially in contrast to the distracting intensity of open-office formats.

Personal-life activities have become more fluid, as well. People
can shop for just about anything anywhere or anytime. They can
contact family members, check their bank accounts, or book res-
ervations all while at the workplace. This fluidity requires workers
and workplaces to make deliberate decisions about boundaries,
both at work and at home. The line between work and personal life
is no longer imposed, as it was in the days when workers "punched
out" on time clocks.

In the past, another fairly clear boundary was between the five-day
workweek and the two-day weekend. That boundary, too, has become more permeable, with more people working on the weekend—
either as regular business hours or on-call time or overtime (whether
paid or not). Sometimes working on weekends is just fine, and some-

times it is not—but in either case, the lack of a clear boundary between work and the rest of one's life can allow work to flow into personal time and swallow up some of those hours that could be spent on more restorative and enjoyable activities.

It used to be that one day of the weekend was a "day of rest"— when there was no work and people observed their religious traditions, often with family gathered together. An innovative proposal is that such a respite be revived as a day of no technology. The author of *24/6: The Power of Unplugging One Day a Week* is herself a technology leader, but has practiced a weekly "tech shabbat" for over ten years. She has this to say about how it protects the personal and play segment of the human renewal cycle from the ever-present onslaught of the digital world:

> Living 24/6 feels like magic, and here's why: it seems to defy the laws of physics, as it both slows down time and gives us more of it. I laugh a lot more on that day without screens. I notice everything in greater detail. I sleep better. It strengthens my relationships and make me feel healthier. It allows me to read, think, be more creative, and reflect in a deeper way. Each week I get a full reset. Afterward, I'm much more productive and efficient, with positive effects that radiate out to the other six days. It even helps renew my appreciation for all that I have access to online, giving me that "Wow, the Internet" realization fresh each week. Who would have thought technology could be more potent in its absence?[14]

But what about when the location of work and home are one and the same? Many writers and therapists work out of their home offices, and some childcare workers open their homes to clients as daycare centers. When military personnel are deployed and living together, their work colleagues are also their roommates, friends, and neighbors. In these sorts of circumstances, difficulties in one domain can easily spill over into the other, as the boundary is non-existent. A different example of the lack of a boundary between work and home comes from people who are aid workers in another country. Burnout is a real risk for aid workers, whose jobs often have them working twelve weeks of fourteen-hour days, then taking a two-week break, then going back at it again. Under conditions like this, as one aid worker explained, a problem such as friction with a supervisor becomes an unrelenting stressor: "We lived in a compound, so you basically lived in the office. The people you hang out with all the time are the people you work with, so everything is intensified, and the lines are blurred. I'd cut myself off from social occasions to avoid having to see my boss."[15]

The distinction between work and home really fell apart in 2020, as the world struggled to find feasible responses to the Covid-19 pandemic. Working from home became a new reality for many employees, and policies on where and when to work shifted dramatically. Workplaces that had insisted on employees working on-site abruptly accepted their working from home as the only means of remaining viable. It was remote work or nothing.

It quickly became clear that remote work was much more feasible than long-standing policies had assumed. It was not everyone's preferred work mode, and for those people who suddenly found themselves caring for young children or overseeing online schooling at home, it was especially challenging. Work requiring direct contact with people suffered, to be sure. Other disappointments might have been due to limitations in the technology or the users' skills, or the value that many people place on being in physical proximity with others. We saw many new variants of burnout being talked about, such as parent burnout, work-from-home burnout, and pandemic burnout. But for other people, working from home turned out to be functional. It saved commuting time, reduced interruptions, and avoided distractions. The experience raised questions about the options that would become available once pandemic restrictions were relaxed as the infection threat receded. Whatever the options might turn out to be, mutual trust will be a must for remote work to be sustainable. Workers need to trust their workplace to expect reasonable levels of productivity, and workplaces need to trust in their employees to devote sufficient energy and attention to getting the work done. As we will see in later chapters, trust is a core value underlying all areas of job-person match.

PROTECTING WORKLOAD FROM INTERFERENCE

With trust and an open, cooperative environment, a workplace can come up with innovative solutions to tackle the problem of workload. The story of how one organization handled it illustrates this well.

The central office of a large university department was the site of many individual workspaces (offices for the administrative leaders, and cubicles for the managerial and clerical staff), but also the site where supplies and equipment were stored, faculty and staff mailboxes were located, and a receptionist welcomed guests and provided basic information and directions. It was, in short, the hub of lots of activity throughout the workday, with people entering, wandering through, and exiting at all times. Often this distracting, sociable climate was enjoyable—as when someone brought by treats to share or told a funny joke—but it also took its toll on productivity. Officially, operations shut down for the lunch hour, noon to one o'clock, but gradually that hour ceased to be a legitimate break for food and relaxation and became instead an hour of intense work to catch up on tasks before the hallway hustle and bustle resumed.

The employees began to complain about the growing workload, which sometimes could not be finished unless they continued to work (on their own time) after the office closed at five o'clock. The supervisor decided that something needed to be done and arranged for everyone to take some time off and get together to explore possible solutions. As the employees vented their frustrations about "all the extra work," they began to realize that the important work had not really expanded, but that they were less able to concentrate on it because of all the interruptions and distractions. They could not tell people to stop collecting their mail, getting supplies, and so on. So, what to do?

The answer they came up with was a "head start" on the day. They proposed that for the first two hours of each workday, from eight to ten in the morning, the central office should be closed to everyone but those who worked there, who would use this uninterrupted and quiet time to make substantial progress on the most important tasks of the day. The office would then open its doors at ten o'clock, ready to receive one and all for whatever other business and socializing was going to be done. By controlling the privacy of the physical office space in this way, the employees were able to achieve a manageable workload. The idea succeeded: faculty and students could easily adjust to the later opening, as could delivery people, and for the rare early-morning visitors, there were signs posted to direct them and provide information.

The lesson of the story is that, with collaboration among the people affected by conditions in a workplace, it is possible to find innovative ways to manage workload (and provide more control, as we will see in the next chapter). True, individuals can come up with personal strategies if left to "do their own thing" to modify their work experience—as long as it doesn't intrude and have a negative impact on others. But more often than not, workers share arrangements with coworkers, and modifications need broader agreement to be implemented successfully.

A second theme is that figuring out what to do about a rising workload does not have to wait until some individuals are at the point of self-diagnosing themselves as burnout cases (or any other worker profile). Any group of colleagues can focus on identifying what could be improved in their workplace, based on a collective evaluation of what the entire group is noticing and experiencing. Attention should be directed not to "the burned-out people in our organization" but to "the risk factors for burnout in our particular workplace." The latter information can then be used to develop customized positive changes, based on everyone's input. Team leaders who take this approach will send a powerful message to employees about how much they are valued for their contributions. Moreover, focusing on what the whole group can do to reduce those risk factors avoids the "blame game" and works instead to promote "what we value in this organization."

Lastly, the successful solution in the story shows that even small changes can be really important, especially if all the relevant people have helped to actually design them. Their personal contribution to the accepted solution will make them more likely to commit to implementing the changes successfully. In many instances, teams and units find that they have more control and flexibility than they realize regarding these small changes, and they can easily be enacted. The office staff's decision to create an early morning period of uninterrupted work time could be implemented with just the approval of their local leader and involved no financial costs.

There is a coda to the story. Years later, the department was moved to a new building (because the old one was being torn down). The new building was designed to have a lot more open workspaces, spread around each floor, with intersecting pathways from one area to another. There were no doors or walls to protect the central office for its quiet and uninterrupted head start—indeed, there was increased foot traffic of people who were not coming "in" to the office, but simply passing through, to go somewhere else. Although the architectural intention was not to prevent the needed privacy, the effect was to do just that.

Workplaces evolve, memories of past problems fade, and good working arrangements do not always endure. This is why it is important that people keep thinking—ideally in collaboration—about risk factors for burnout. And, as we will see in chapters to come, some improvements can be more serendipitous or result from trial-and-error approaches to improve things, and grow to be widely recognized as good solutions.

5

Control

More than fifty years ago, the idea was developed that managers take very different approaches to their employees based on which of two basic theories of human motivation they subscribe to—"Theory X" or "Theory Y." Managers who operate by Theory X hold a more negative view of workers, assuming that they don't have much ambition, cannot handle responsibilities, are lazy, and are only doing the job to earn money. They assume that workers are mostly self-interested and not motivated to perform beyond the minimum level required to keep their jobs. These Theory X assumptions lead managers to a hands-on approach of close supervision, because they don't trust the workers to do a good job. Determined to exercise tight control, they are on the lookout for mistakes and quick to penalize them. In contrast, managers who operate by Theory Y have a more positive view of workers, assuming that they are intrinsically motivated by the work and will embrace the responsibility to do the job well. In this case, managers check in with workers but don't feel the need to supervise them strictly. They allow them more autonomy in completing tasks, and they tend to relate to workers in a more personal, teaching-based manner. The particulars of these two management styles may differ by the type of occupation or work product, and by the manager's personality, but in general the Theory X style is more associated with worker burnout.[1]

In this chapter, we move into the second area of job-person matches and mismatches: the degree to which workers feel a sense of *control*, can act with *autonomy*, and are granted *flexibility*.

Control

Very few workplaces, of course, operate as democracies in which everyone has an equal voice in consequential decisions. In almost all of them, employers hold substantially more power than employees. The owners, CEOs, middle managers, and supervisors who constitute the chain of command get to determine who does what and when, and how they should do whatever that may be. Their authority is legitimized by the governance structure of the organization. So any attempt by a worker to gain more control does not start on a level playing field. Yet employers also have the prerogative to allocate more authority further down the line. The question, then, is how much have they allocated to workers in a given job? What latitude do individuals have to accomplish objectives in the way they think best?

Frustration with having insufficient control over one's work is an important indication of a job-person mismatch. People want the opportunity to make choices and decisions, to use their ability and training to think and to solve problems, and to have some input in the process of achieving the outcomes for which they will be held accountable. Lack of control is often a more serious issue for workers than workload per se. It can easily lead to a sense of inefficacy and cynicism about both the adequacy of job processes and the ultimate value of one's work output. Stated in more positive terms, when employees do perceive that they can exercise professional judgment, and have access to the resources necessary to do their work well, they are more likely to experience engagement. There is a world of difference between personal accountability and forced adherence to rigid policies and tight monitoring.

Policies that impose narrow constraints on how work is done—cookie-cutter, one-size-fits-all processes to be followed—allow no room for judgment or innovation and leave workers feeling less responsible for their outcomes, not more. Mechanical management leads to mechanical performance. Similarly, close monitoring of staff performance has human costs beyond the supervisors' time and energies, in that it diminishes the capacity of employees to adapt and take initiative when that is required. This style of supervision sends the demeaning message that "you can't be trusted." It says that management doesn't respect your judgment, or doesn't consider you very smart, or doesn't believe you will stay on task.

When greater control is allocated to individuals in workplaces, it's because managers are satisfied on two points of consideration: productivity and trust. They need to know, first, that people are willing and able to produce sufficient output before they will grant them greater discretion over where, when, and how they work. Beyond worrying about productivity suffering, they also want assurance that allocating more authority to workers will not open the door to bad behaviors. They may suspect that, with greater discretion, workers will start cutting corners on quality, or undermining the efforts of colleagues they dislike, or diverting resources away from workplace priorities. No one would deny that problems can occur when managers delegate and disappear. The challenge is finding the right balance between abdicating managerial responsibility and insisting on making all decisions.

When the Covid-19 pandemic abruptly shifted businesses and other organizations around the world to work-from-home arrangements, many employees gained a sense of control they had never experienced before in their workplaces. And research shows that, despite the anxieties and challenges of the time, productivity rose under the remote-work conditions.[2] The prospect began to be widely discussed that many employers might never go back to their pre-pandemic insistence that workers be physically present in office buildings. For managers disinclined to cede control, that would not be a welcome development.

A hint of this attitude comes through in a *Washington Post* guest editorial authored by the chief executive of Washingtonian Media, which publishes the city-focused magazine *The Washingtonian*.[3] The gist of the op-ed was that employees should understand, if remote-work arrangements became the norm for many of them, their organizations would be much worse off—and if performance declined they would be pushed toward cost-cutting. The CEO extolled the value of spontaneous conversations, mentoring of younger staff, and workplace "citizenship behaviors"—all the informal acts by which people contribute to an organization's smooth functioning beyond the strict fulfillment of their job requirements. But despite the general tone of employee appreciation, she chose to end the piece on an ominous note: "So although there might be some pains and anxiety going back into the office, the biggest benefit for workers may be simple job security. Remember something every manager knows: The hardest people to let go are the ones you know."

Employees of *The Washingtonian* reacted immediately to what could be read as a message to them: Get back to your desks or you're fired. It didn't help that the headline originally used for the piece was "As a CEO, I Want My Employees to Understand the Risks of Not Returning to Work in the Office." The following morning, more than a dozen of them tweeted: "As members of the Washingtonian editorial staff, we want our CEO to understand the risks of not valuing our labor. We are dismayed by CM's public threat to our livelihoods. We will not be publishing today."[4] The CEO hastened to assure them that she intended no such threat. But that final line was at least a frank reminder of who in an organization has most control over people's work: the manager with the power to end their employment.

If bosses make broad statements about subjects as important as people's need for control over their lives, then those bosses should know that their own employees will be sensitive to the message. As a parallel, in our own work as university professors, we learned long ago not to make jokes about how grades are determined. For students, grades are serious business—a consequential area where someone else's extreme power diminishes their own control over outcomes. They are not a joking matter—no more than job security is.

Autonomy

The importance of personal autonomy cannot be overstated. Having the sense of being able to make one's own choices based on one's own beliefs and priorities is at the core of human dignity. The word *autonomy* is Latin for *self-rule* and can apply at many levels—from countries and regions to organizations, teams, and individuals. At the personal level, it can refer to the capacity of individuals to act independently and to make their own informed decisions in any domain of life. In workplaces, it means feeling capable of doing a good job and being able to take action as needed to correct things that go wrong and adjust to changing circumstances. This does not imply that people prefer working entirely by themselves, believe they should make decisions in isolation of others working in the same context, or are resistant to feedback. Rather, it means they want to operate with an amount of discretion and responsibility that recognizes their capability.

There are many ways in which people can gain and sustain personal autonomy in the workplace. Obviously, a first step involves training processes and the successful attainment of relevant skills as measured by certain standards. But once that fundamental capability has been established, what else is required for a worker to step up to making informed suggestions or criticisms, or pursuing independent innovations, or taking on new responsibilities? Regular and open dialogues among employees and team members and managers are critical for enhancing a sense of job autonomy and job satisfaction for everyone. Such dialogues have to be mutual, two-way conversations, in which everyone has opportunities to ask questions or suggest answers—so a shared sense of psychological safety is also necessary. Managers can do several things to enhance employees' autonomy and control, such as clarify expectations, ask for ideas about what could be improved or fixed, and agree to advocate for needed resources or procedural changes.

In some cases, people may be well trained and highly motivated, but chronic obstacles may still make it difficult for them to work with autonomy in the jobs they are qualified to do. A roadblock may be internal or external, but if the effect is to erode the control that people have over their job, it threatens both the integrity of their work and the pride they take in it.

As a prime example, consider the rules and regulations that have been established in many professions to ensure certain positive outcomes or to prevent negative ones. These can also become frustrating sources of delay and difficulty: they don't always apply to the situations workers face, and they can slow down or reduce the achievement of required outcomes. For healthcare employees, for example, working with medical insurance regulations is a major source of stress. We've heard them complain that "this stuff interferes with my ability to provide treatment," citing time wasted on excessive prior-authorization processes and denials of standard-of-care practices. Also typical was the resentment voiced that "some reviewer in some company who doesn't know the client and who has less training than I do decides how many therapy sessions the client can get from me." This isn't just an irritating setback. The real problem is the therapist's feeling that "I no longer have control over the type and quality of care I provide." Such issues are far beyond the power of individual workers to change, but senior leadership across many parallel institutions could organize to challenge and modify these larger barriers.

Perhaps most often, control mismatches flare up within supervisory relationships. When things are going well, supervisors allocate autonomy and discretion to employees whom they trust. That is, supervisors give more latitude to employees in whom they have confidence regarding their abilities and willingness to pursue workplace priorities. When trust is lacking, they monitor employees' decisions more closely.

In some settings, the latitude supervisors can give to their employees is constrained by policies or contract provisions. The supervisors lack the authority to allocate autonomy to individual employees or to work groups on definitive actions such as closing sales, selecting treatments, or developing curriculum elements. An important step toward reducing mismatches is locating the problem. Is it in the supervisory relationship itself, or further up the line in workplace policy?

The varying power that supervisors exercise in allocating autonomy was on full display in 2021, as Covid-19 infection rates began to drop and pandemic controls were relaxed. Many people who had found working from home to be more productive saw the transition as an opportunity to negotiate their ideal balance of on-site and remote work. For some, the modifications that could be made turned out to be dictated by global workplace policies. Others could negotiate workable solutions tailored to their unique job requirements and teamwork expectations, and the authority to bless any modified work arrangements lay with their immediate supervisors.

Either condition can lead to a better match on autonomy, but the routes toward it differ. When supervisors have discretion, the path to resolving mismatches can be simpler and quicker. On the other hand, a personal process with an immediate supervisor is prone to break down when there is mistrust or animosity in the supervisory relationship. Meanwhile, anyone who has been involved in developing workplace policies knows it can be a slow and complex process. The latter route has an advantage, however, in that policy resolutions, once enacted, apply broadly and instantly.

A technology innovation firm was undergoing a major transition as a result of growth based on financial success. The employees were dedicated to their work and to the company but were experiencing serious frustration in the projects they undertook. The survey assessment revealed that the most common result was for employees to fall into the ineffective profile (because their most negative scores were in professional inefficacy). Although their dedication to the organization was evident in the strong match on values, there was a serious mismatch on control (and to a lesser extent, both reward and fairness). Employees' ratings were critical of the supervision they were receiving (which connected to their issues with control and autonomy) and indicated that they saw things overall as changing for the worse.

The written comments on the survey confirmed a general view that the root of the problem was the imposition of central management controls as the company had grown. The CEO, a dynamic and inspirational leader, had developed the company based on autonomous project teams that worked a new idea through the concept phase, the development of investment funds, and the prototype process to the point that it was ready for production. The CEO managed the complex work of the organization through direct interactions with team leaders. Based on quick weekly meetings, he would update the project management documents on the computer. With this framework the company successfully took several projects to market and built a group of dedicated and capable employees.

But with the growth of the company, the scope of projects exceeded this personal level of management. The board of the company brought in a management consulting firm to establish management control and accounting procedures to keep systematic track of a wide variety of projects dispersed over the various sites where the company did its work. The systems were effective in tracking the important business information, but they placed constraints on employees while increasing their paperwork.

Thus, the procedures that were supposed to make things better were actually generating a serious mismatch between the level of control that employees had and what they wanted. To deal with this mismatch, the company established an in-house task force on management systems to study the growing literature on management transitions in quickly growing companies. The task force provided senior management with contact information on major consultants in this field. Their recommendation was that the company embark on a collaborative process aimed at developing a workable management system that would result in an integrated, successful corporation supporting the innovative initiatives of the employees. This solution offered the autonomy employees desired.

Flexibility

A key principle for enhancing a better job-person match in control is flexibility. There are several meanings of this term, all of which are highly relevant. First, flexibility refers to the quality of bending easily without breaking. This stands in contrast to the basic engineering concepts of both stress (the force experienced by an object which causes a change in it) and stress tests (the conditions under which the object will ultimately break). These engineering concepts are usually applied to technology or infrastructure (such as bridges or power grids), but the parallel to the human body has been instructive. Conditions that allow people to bend and withstand stressors, rather than break in terms of poor health and well-being, are worth pursuing. Indeed, that is the basic rationale underlying the notion of a better match or fit between the job and the person.

Second, flexibility refers to the ability to be easily modified. This means that some things are not static and permanent but can be changed and revised; people can choose to do things differently. When workers can get out of a rut or can modify the "same old, same old" routine, they are able to exercise some autonomy and feel more in control of their jobs. Sometimes major tasks can be done differently, such as developing a new sales pitch, but even more ordinary everyday tasks can be handled in new ways, such as responding to email requests, or greeting customers, or writing the opening paragraph of a report. Such modifications can be an ongoing process, and individual workers can often do them on their own. By reevaluating the many aspects of their job and focusing on those where they have some choice and discretion, they can then modify, vary, shift, or reorganize how they handle their workday.

Third, flexibility refers to the willingness to change or compromise. This means that everyone—workers, teams, management— is ready and prepared to seek better solutions than the ones that already exist. Usually this requires joint efforts between these various groups to determine better ways in which the work will get done.

Increasingly, flexibility has become a necessity for employees in today's workforce, as they try to balance their jobs with the needs of their nonwork lives. Some of those needs may be fixed (children's school hours do not match those of the workplace), but others may be random or unexpected (a health problem requires seeing a doctor). The importance of flexible work options became even more apparent during the Covid-19 pandemic, when many office jobs had to be done from home, and the usual hours and operating procedures changed. People came up with new ways of doing their jobs, which may help them work better in the post-pandemic era. Remote work is likely to continue in the future, so companies might accommodate a broader mix of people being off-site going forward. Also, some of the tasks that did not get done during shutdowns may not need to be done at all (remember the subtraction of clutter?). Workplaces will have to evolve in additional ways to ensure that they are safe and healthy environments (whether physical or virtual) in which people do their jobs. All of this means that flexibility is going to continue to be a key factor in achieving good job-person matches in the future world of work.

An example of a workplace that offered a bit more flexibility was a hospital that had conducted a survey of physicians to identify key risk factors for burnout. Several interesting findings from this effort prompted new ideas about possible corrective actions. The most intriguing result, however, was a discrepancy between responses in the area of control. Almost all of the physicians reported negative scores of mismatch on this dimension—but one subgroup of specialists did not. Instead, its members reported positive scores on control. What was going on with them? Through follow-up discussions it was discovered that this subgroup used a different system for scheduling, which generated a work schedule for each doctor but then allowed the recipients to accept or refuse what was offered to them. The central system used by the rest of the subgroups allowed for no such pushback—its communication was more like "here's your schedule; get on with it." This one feature was the key to turning a mismatch into a match: the doctors who could interact with their scheduling system and make a change said this extra bit of control gave them much-needed latitude as they juggled demands of work life and personal life.

It turned out that this scheduling system could work well for other specialties but that it would require the hospital to devote staff time to scheduling, to accommodate the dialogue that followed a physician refusing the initial schedule. The payoff for that additional staffing investment would be a greater sense of control and fewer indicators of burnout for the physicians. With doctors being the highest-paid professionals and the costliest to recruit, the math worked out in favor of increasing the resources devoted to scheduling.

However, the fact that a system could be redesigned to make an actual positive difference opened everybody's thinking about addressing control issues. The success of the different system was a concrete example of "it can be done"—and helped stimulate some other suggestions for improving the scheduling process.

TENTATIVE RELATIONSHIPS

It is important to acknowledge another aspect of workplaces in the twenty-first century: the relationship of people with workplaces has become increasingly tentative.[5] A "job for life" has become an outmoded concept in much of the world, employer-based pensions have faded,[6] and workplaces shift their liabilities toward individual employees. As a result, people need to attend to managing their current job in the context of their career. A long-term perspective has benefits, but it introduces uncertainty. In addition to control problems within their job, people contend with challenges to exercising control over their future careers.

The twenty-first century has a tentative quality to it, promoting background anxiety. It is a world of disposable items. Many items are not repairable, and if they are, the repairs would cost more than buying a replacement item. It is better to throw them away when they stop working so well. Much of what previously were considered permanent items—books, music, pictures—are now ethereal patterns of electronic data. Applications that were previously owned turned into subscriptions. Things are not only less concrete, but they also prompt less commitment.

When people have a more tentative relationship with their job, it goes against their developing a sense of control of their work. People become more cautious. They have fewer options for participating in major developments at a workplace. In short, it is difficult to exercise control in a relationship without confidence that the relationship will continue.

With the acknowledgment of this reality in the workplace, we must remember that the control area of work life has a foundational role in the relationships people develop with their job. Greater control increases the potential for developing good matches with other areas of work life. The capacity to make decisions regarding tasks, access to resources, and team membership has implications for managing workload, finding a compatible community, and emphasizing valued activities. With the capacity to participate in decisions or to make choices, people can adjust to whatever comes their way. Employees are also more likely to stay in their jobs when they have autonomy and flexibility.

Supervisor relationships have a pivotal role in determining employees' possibilities for fulfilling matches at work. Policies that allocate authority to supervisors allow them to accommodate a variety of working styles and preferences. In the context of responsive relationships between supervisors and employees, people can resolve issues promptly in ways that recognize diverse perspectives on the strains and opportunities that shape life at work. Smooth and ongoing communication from supervisors with managers helps to maintain unity and purpose in the workplace. Supervisors need to know that management backs the choices they make in developing their work groups.

The supervisory relationship is not only central to autonomy and control. As we will see in Chapter 6, it also has much to do with achieving a good match regarding rewards. In fact, rewards are a means of controlling what people do at work, even if, as positive incentives, they have an upside to them. But the effects of rewards are also complicated by their pervasive nature, in that they don't only come from people in positions of greater authority. As the next chapter reveals, the most meaningful forms of recognition may come from peers or from the work itself.

6

Rewards

The word *reward* may bring to mind cash for a safe return of a lost item, or a treat to a dog after sitting and staying. Or you might think of rewards as something you earn in the workplace for tasks accomplished. Whether they are given in return for something received, after a desired response, or for a job well done, these benefits are positive and usually result in a greater understanding of what is expected and desired going forward.

Beyond their tangible benefits, rewards make a real difference in people's lives because of the positive feedback they convey. Insufficient or poorly designed recognition and rewards (whether social, financial, or institutional) increase people's vulnerability to burnout, because these devalue both the work and the workers. Low rewards are also closely associated with feelings of inefficacy. The causal directions are likely mixed: unrewarding work can make people feel exhausted or cynical; and feeling exhausted or cynical can make work feel unrewarding. Feelings and rewards maintain a balance. Improving the level of reward has potential to increase energy, involvement, and efficacy.

We can learn a great deal about the social domain of a workplace through its rewards. For instance, if a compensation system focuses on individual achievement versus group achievement, it is a fundamental statement on the nature of the company. It makes one statement about power if allocation of rewards is an open, objective process, and a different statement if the allocation is a closely guarded decision by top executives. Management has the capacity and authority to allocate rewards to shape behavior toward its objectives. Employees lack a complementary way to shape management actions. The positions of workplaces on these critical questions of rewards also have direct implications for employees' potential to experience sufficient belonging and autonomy, which in turn have consequences for the prevalence of burnout. We've found that the presence of positive feedback, an important kind of reward, is prominent for employees who feel engaged, and often minimal or absent for those who align with either the burnout or the ineffective profile, regardless of how well they have done their jobs.

Understanding what gratifies and what irritates regarding rewards can save workplaces a great deal of time and trouble. Once it becomes clear through surveys or conversations that the reward area of work life has problems, it's possible to identify what changes would make a difference. People do not automatically embrace reward systems. To resonate with people, it is important that awards or celebrations fit with other aspects of their lives and have credibility.

As an organization designs its customized rewards system, credibility is of paramount importance. People are more likely to buy into an award if the process is transparent—that is, if they can see who is being considered, who is doing the consideration, and the criteria upon which the decision is made. An open process reduces suspicions of favoritism. People usually judge that they are working capably and can be reluctant to accept that others are doing better. The use of group versus individual awards is another important dimension of a credible system. Much of what is produced in contemporary workplaces results from group efforts. Giving an award to one or a few individuals in a larger group can dissipate the impact of that positive attention. By the same token, if workers' rewards are to be contingent on others' efforts, they need to accept that their contributions and success are highly mutually dependent. Rewards need to reflect the reality of the value-creation process.

We've found that two aspects of rewards have especially strong implications for the phenomenon of burnout. The first is whether they are considered fair. Are people confident that the system rewards what it claims to reward? As Chapter 8 will explore more deeply, unfair treatment encourages people to withdraw psychologically, with greater risk of becoming cynical. The second is whether rewards are inherent in the work. As people perform their day-to-day job tasks, is the act of completing those rewarding in itself? If so, that has a pervasive impact on their sense of engagement. Managers of workplaces should recognize these all-important aspects with a carefully thought-out and executed strategy for rewards—and may be relieved to learn they can address many issues with adjustments that are not strictly about financial remuneration.

Appreciation

Expressing appreciation is the way people reward one another at work. In fact, social recognition is one of the most important and meaningful rewards for all employees. To hear from someone else—a colleague, a client, a customer—that one has done something that made a positive difference and is appreciated by others can truly make one's day.

Receiving good vibes or compliments from others is an uplifting experience—but so, too, is expressing them to others. Simply thinking appreciative thoughts moves only a small way down the road. Maintaining a culture of appreciation requires explicit words and actions that convey messages to others that their contributions are noted. Expressing appreciation has a performative quality, as well. Others observe the act of gratitude, see its effects, and are prompted to act similarly. To build a culture of appreciation requires mutual participation, with everyone thriving as both source and recipient of everyday acts of kindness. Saying thanks or acting in ways that explicitly acknowledge a colleague's contribution has a direct positive effect on that person but also resonates more broadly.

The source of recognition—whether it comes from management or from colleagues—also makes a difference. Each brings something of value. Management recognition of accomplishments or contributions is understood to have career or promotion implications beyond the affirmation of the particular recognition. But not all important accolades are showered down from above. Appreciation among colleagues has its own powerful impact. Praise expressed by colleagues has a less official, more spontaneous and sincere quality that makes it something more special. Colleagues' compliments can also be more meaningful, given that they are often more familiar with the fine points of a job and better positioned to see who does it well. This underscores why any effort to enhance the rewarding qualities of a workplace should be collaborative. Approaches drawing on more people's input have a greater chance of focusing on what really matters and coming up with solutions that are credible. With a broad base of genuine participation, any new reward scheme is more likely to take hold in the organization.

An important yet often overlooked part of organizational culture is the emotional tone of the workplace. What is the overall feeling of being there? Is it joyful, energized, tense, dispirited? Although this may sound ethereal, what psychologists call the affective climate of a social setting is something people reliably pick up on. It transmits through the social encounters that occur throughout the workday. It therefore makes up part of the rewards environment, as the satisfaction of a job well done can go deeper when it is shared with others. And disappointment can be heavier when people must carry it on their own.

Extrinsic Rewards

Money matters. For most people, work is the way to get money. They need to support their current life expenses while (hopefully) putting some aside for special occasions, emergencies, and retirement. While employees may not be in it only for the money, they do need the money. People need salaries in accordance with their contribution. They need the benefits and the status that employment provides. In the United States (and in many developing countries), employees need gainful employment to have access to a level of health care that most of the developed world considers to be a human right. It's been said that being a park ranger pays people in beautiful sunsets, and no doubt those are an enjoyable and enriching part of doing that work. But sunsets do not pay the bills, provide health care, or advance expertise. So, although it is important that work be meaningful, meaning alone is not enough. Even the finest job is work much of the time, and people require (and sometimes thrive on) increased compensation.

Workplaces express their values through financial rewards, in the forms of salaries and commissions, benefits with clear cash value, and bonuses and other special awards. Employees attend closely to financial distinctions with a critical eye to interpret their standing vis-à-vis others in the workplace. When compensation is supposed to reflect differences in performance or responsibilities, people question how performance is measured. Workplaces must contend with challenges to justify differences in these extrinsic rewards. It is important to acknowledge that there is an inherent self-serving bias. People tend to think well of themselves. Their inclination is to be skeptical about reward allocations that favor others. They may eventually agree with the allocation, but their agreement does not go without saying. It can take some convincing. Further, performance measurement is difficult. Many jobs are complex mixtures of components, some of which can only be assessed subjectively. Great performance on one part can coexist with modest or poor performance on another.

Also important to recognize is that reward allocation occurs against a socioeconomic background—in many countries, a context of increasing income inequality and concentration of wealth. Increasing proportions of business profits go to capital investors, with less going to labor. Ironically, more money goes to entities that don't spend money but invest it. As investments in property increase the costs of housing, it becomes more expensive for employees to live within commuting distances of workplaces. As a result, few people can afford not to note how their extrinsic rewards measure up. They have an ongoing and compelling interest in growing them.

People aspire to find a balance between the effort they put into a job and the rewards the job provides. That seems entirely reasonable, but sustaining that balance presents challenges. Research has confirmed that effort / reward imbalances are bad for workers' well-being, while satisfactory balances encourage work engagement.[1] For example, when people perceive that they are putting in more effort than they're getting credit for, they feel resentful and exploited. They are inclined to reduce their contributions if they can't get raises or more fulfilling assignments.

One source of complexity in the effort / reward balance is that whether it is satisfactory depends on what is happening with other people. Although someone may be content with a given balance of effort to reward, that contentment may be in jeopardy if it becomes evident that others are receiving similar rewards for noticeably less effort, or greater rewards for the same effort. That perception prompts concerns about fairness and respect. People may read such imbalances as unjustified criticism of their performance. Known wage gaps or opportunity gaps cause people to question their standing as full members of their workplace communities. A difference in rewards not only thwarts a worker's sense of belonging but challenges that person's fundamental identity. To add injury to insult, it slashes earnings potential in the long term. Emotional turmoil caused by rewards concern has the effect of sapping energy and driving exhaustion. The message of exclusion implicit in lower rewards prompts people to reciprocate by distancing themselves. Lower compensation implies that a person's contributions and competence are of lower value, undermining the sense of efficacy. In short, a rewards mismatch is a multifaceted push toward burnout.

One of us, in our idealistic youth, worked for a time in a small nonprofit where, for a few years, everyone received the same pay. That situation reduced the effort / reward calculation to an effort-only variable, so it was easier to get a sense of whether people were pulling their weight. But in almost all workplaces, pay varies as well as effort, leaving people confused and doubtful about the reasonableness or fairness of rewards differences. Regardless of whether compensation is open or secret, as people perceive differences they develop theories to explain them. These theories may put the employer in a bad light, attributing nefarious practices. Open, honest communication about pay systems and the rationales for adjusting compensation can avoid unproductive speculation and distress.

At a company in its fourth year of operation, an employment survey revealed a serious mismatch on rewards. In the business of creating computer-based professional development courses for corporate customers, the company had started out strong and grown quickly from a ten-person operation to employ some three hundred employees. But it had encountered a crisis as people increasingly showed signs of burnout. Heading into the survey, leaders of the company anticipated it would highlight problems in the area of workload, but this did not turn out to be the case. Although the staff worked long hours, they did not experience workload as a mismatch. They accepted long hours as unavoidable, especially as program deadlines approached. They had, however, expected their employment to be much more financially rewarding by this time. Instead, the costs and cash flow problems associated with the company's quick and constant expansion prevented staff from reaping the anticipated financial gains. What's more, while the employees had a strong sense of community at their workplace, many did not see their immediate supervisors as part of that. The responses overall did not suggest enthusiasm for the organization or its management.

In the past, management had attempted to allay people's financial concerns through a series of presentations on the company's finances. The presentations explained the current cash-flow constraints but ended with optimistic projections of how the company's fortunes would change. Much to the disappointment of management, however, the response to these presentations was increased cynicism. "They're always painting this rosy picture about how well the company is doing, and how we're going to share in the wealth, but I have yet to see a dime of this supposed good fortune." Employees who had been with the company since its early days feared that the larger company had lost its initial commitment to the people who had realized its potential through their hard work. Newer staff members had seen little evidence of organizational values tending toward shared gains. Both groups had concluded that, despite considerable talk around the company about its commitment to profit-sharing, it lacked a solid commitment to practicing what it preached.

In response to these survey findings, the company formalized its commitment to profit-sharing through a new financing plan. Although the payout was more modest than originally projected, it was real. The employees' confidence in the company grew and their cynicism decreased.

As we've seen, extrinsic rewards can also, by affirming employees' sense of accomplishment, have the effect of strengthening efficacy. Although people generally have a good sense of whether they are performing well or struggling with their work, they also interpret external recognition of their contributions as meaningful indicators of their competence. Experiencing a sense of mastery and also having one's success extrinsically rewarded makes for a strong combination. It contributes to an enduring sense of self-efficacy that people can continue to draw on as they take on greater challenges or work to recover from setbacks.[2]

Intrinsic Rewards

As with personal relationships, people's relationships with their workplaces go far beyond simple transactions, like exchanging work for money. Sustainable relationships with work are ones that meet psychological needs. Often these gains come through the intrinsic rewards of doing work that needs to be done. When doing their work opens opportunities for initiative, people experience more *autonomy*. When doing their work entails positive social encounters with respected others, people feel a sense of *belonging*. And when doing their work conveys a sense of accomplishment and self-efficacy, people experience greater *competence*. Humans are profoundly motivated by the pursuit of these core needs, and to have any of them more fulfilled counts as a rewarding experience.

A brief story of how one workplace improved recognition shows how doing so can foster a stronger sense of community. In a university department, there was a tradition by which the faculty hosted an annual spring picnic to honor the staff. Everyone would gather in a local park, the professors would grill hamburgers and serve food to the administrative employees, and afterward there were presentations of special pins to mark milestones of service—for example, when someone had worked in the department for ten years. The outings were pleasant (even if a few faculty members missed the point that they were supposed to be doing the cooking and serving), and the picnics continued for many years.

The position of department chair rotated among the faculty every five years, and when a new professor took on the job, she set up regular meetings with the staff to check in and find out how things were going for them. As spring approached, she asked the staff how they felt about the upcoming picnic—and their answer was, "not so great." Although it was a department tradition, it did not actually convey a sense of thanks for the staff's work, or recognition of when it went above and beyond the call of duty (as when a professor came in late with a task that had to be finished that day).

As she heard this sentiment expressed a few times, the chair started asking, "What should we do instead? We really do want to offer a special thank you, so what would communicate that better?" The staff were at first surprised but then delighted to be asked, and they soon came up with a two-part suggestion. First, they wondered, could the lunch be held in a nicer location than the park, and could it be potluck, with everyone bringing good food, and perhaps better beverages than canned soft drinks? And second, could the department's money therefore saved on frozen hamburgers and tubs of potato salad be spent instead on some improvements to the staff lounge or people's workstations?

The chair said "Yes!"—and in that first year, the money was spent on some new carpeting in the staff lounge, and one of the employees volunteered her nearby apartment for what turned out to be a more pleasant and delicious lunch for everyone. Even more importantly, the revised lunch format changed the dynamics between the staff and the faculty. Instead of being two sides defined by their job titles, they could all just interact as adults who were enjoying each other's company, getting to know each other better, and having a good time at a party. In terms of the food, everyone contributed and everyone was served. People made new connections based on shared interests (hiking, making ceramics, playing basketball), or having children in the same school, or liking the same movies, and so forth. Getting better acquainted as individuals with lives outside the workplace allowed interactions back in the department office to take on a more collegial and friendly tone. This new tradition of a party plus a gift to improve the staff's work environment was not only more meaningful and well received, but had the ripple effect of improving the social climate of the department.

Sometimes, an individual's sense of fulfillment comes down to how much they feel they are exercising established skills and developing new ones. Learning and honing a capability often makes a practical contribution to one's career potential and financial rewards in the long run, but it is also a source of intrinsic satisfaction. Fulfillment at work can also benefit from greater breadth as well as depth. While deepening one's specialization and practicing skills provide a sense of mastery, opportunities to participate in diverse projects can foster a growth mindset and keep one open to new experiences.

We also believe fulfillment at work is closely linked with hope. At work, people look to the future and want their careers to be going somewhere. While they look to the past for context to interpret events, they look to the future to evaluate whether their efforts are worthwhile. Experiencing fulfillment in autonomy, belonging, and competence confirms that you're doing something right today and that you're in the right place to be doing it. The future looks brighter. In the immediate moment, this can produce the ideal day-to-day experience of *flow*: the condition of being fully absorbed in the task at hand. The flow state produces enjoyment in the moment while also giving people the energized focus to exert their most creative and productive efforts. Operating in a flow state, a person does deep work that goes beyond meeting minimal standards to create output of exceptional quality.[3]

Money, as good as it might be, is just not enough. Although essential to a viable work life, financial compensation does not provide the social status of public recognition, the sense of belonging from appreciative words, or the fulfillment of work that gives a sense of flow. For people to thrive they need multiple forms of recognition. Any workplace that fails to provide opportunities for a wide range of positive responses will be severely challenged to maintain an engaged workforce.

Moving toward better rewards matches need not require drastic action. Often, nuanced refinements in the current design of structures and processes can make a big difference in building cohesive communities and enhancing people's lives at work. As a first step in taking action with respect to social support and recognition, find out what irritant bothers the most people most of the time—the chronic "pebble in their shoe"—and what is already working well.

Rewards and recognition come primarily from people. The prevalence of appreciation and support in day-to-day encounters plays a defining role in workplace culture. These are important points to keep in mind as we move to a chapter exploring the most important way that healthy workplaces fulfill workers' needs for belonging. As we will see, the degree to which a person feels supported by a workplace community shapes much of what happens in other areas of work life.

7

Community

Workplaces are social constructions. People invented them, codified them into law, invested money, time, and talent into them, and have operated them for days, years, or centuries. The invention of the corporation moved many workplaces out of the personal domain of a founder's possession into a realm of entities that exceed human life spans. Within that expansive framework, workplace processes are inherently social. Behind and beside any high-profile person are others attending to the nitty-gritty, preparing the stage. It is hard to imagine an Academy Awards acceptance speech beginning with, "I accept this Oscar for what I achieved all on my own, with no help from anyone!"

The quality of the relationships among employees on the job constitutes the community bedrock of all the work profiles. To have a sense of belonging, people need more than the simple proximity of others, and feeling merely accepted does not suffice. Belonging depends on behavior from others that includes and supports one's participation in the life of the workplace. This truth of all job settings takes on extra significance when the critical work has to be done by teams. A positive workplace culture is built upon active civility among all employees and their colleagues, in words and in deeds. Another critical aspect of a positive workplace community is the active provision of social support, with people knowing they can turn to others for advice and help when they need it, and in turn providing that needed assistance to their colleagues. Mutual respect, responsiveness, and trust are essential for these mutually supporting behaviors to take place.

The dynamics of workplaces go far beyond the dictates of job requirements, also encompassing employees' sense of belonging in these communities. The quality of openness and supportiveness of a workplace community may reflect a work group's history, the qualities of its leadership, and the kinds of challenges people engage with in their work. People do not relinquish their personal identities when entering work domains. They continue to be unique individuals made up of varying characteristics and backgrounds, diverse in their genders, religions, culture, homelands, and political alliances. Employers and employees may be barred from considering some of those characteristics in work decisions and actions—for example, an employer cannot consider a person's race in making a hiring decision, and an employee cannot invoke a cultural norm as a reason to disrespect a customer. But despite these enforced policies and values, personal characteristics often do play a role in the relationships of people with their workplaces and among the people within those workplaces.

In parallel with a personal identity, every employee takes on a work identity. Job descriptions define who people are at work— sometimes strictly, sometimes loosely—by clarifying their roles, their tasks, and their areas of authority. Whether we're talking about a teacher, a doctor, an engineer, a CEO, or a custodian, the job provides the incumbent with an identity and a set of people with whom they interact. It attaches the worker to the workplace in a specific way that conveys who they are, what skills and perspectives they bring to the table, and in what ways they will contribute.

To varying degrees, workplaces have identities based on a culture with values, aspirations, and a sense of their place in the pantheon of workplaces. To varying degrees, so do people. Respect becomes a quality of communities when these identities are mutually accepted and reflected in encounters of people and workplaces. The "mutually accepted" condition is essential. People can have what they consider to be perfectly reasonable expectations of their workplaces—and vice versa, workplaces can have expectations that seem reasonable to place on people—but these can come to naught if they are not reciprocated. If either side rejects the other's view of the relationship, things go poorly.

For example, consider three comments made by people working in a British hospital. One employee made this complaint: "The culture is extremely difficult. We are treated like schoolchildren and are also called that. There is no flexibility of working hours—even though, when interviewing for the position, we were told that there *would* be flexibility. Nine employees in my group have resigned in less than a year due to high volume of work and no flexibility." Another employee had this to say: "Management treats staff unfairly and favors certain staff as they are mates. No scope for development. No transparency. Treated like children, no respect. No innovation and dynamic leadership. Lack of open communication, and management is not accessible." Finally, consider what one manager said about the staff, and how it connects to the previous statements: "Staff are usually okay until you question their work. Moody and childish reactions are quite common." Clearly, this is a workplace in which staff and management need to work on establishing a greater foundation of mutual respect.

Civility

Given the variety of people in a workplace, and the potential for clashes among them based on both their personal and work identities, what is the social glue that binds them together into a well-functioning and productive job community? The answer is *civility*. From the Latin word *civilis*—relating to public life or befitting a citizen—it has always meant treating others with respect and politeness, even kindness and friendliness. More recently, definitions of civility have shifted to a greater emphasis on respect: "Civility involves treating others with dignity, acting with regard to others' feelings, and preserving the social norms for mutual respect."[1]

Five actions define civility in workplace social encounters, by confirming an identity of belonging to the workplace community. These five actions are: awareness, acknowledgment, acceptance, appreciation, and accommodation.

The minimal level of civility is becoming aware of another person. At times, people not only act as if they were unaware of another person's existence; they never actually registered the other person's presence. Without *awareness*, nothing good can come of the encounter.

Acknowledgment goes a step beyond awareness, requiring action. Acknowledging can be as subtle as a word, a gesture, or just a nod, especially if those involved have a solid foundation to their relationship. Lacking a solid foundation, minimal acknowledging may come across as dismissive. When people feel uncertain about their status or level of acceptance within workplace communities, more definitive acknowledgment can provide some needed confirmation.

Acceptance actively includes someone in the community's activities. It is one thing to have an official position in a workplace; it is another to have colleagues sharing information and attending to one another in ways that signal one's full membership in its decisions and events. Being left out of processes or informal gatherings isolates a worker from a workplace community, but active inclusion in these events provides valued confirmation of status.

Appreciation provides another dimension to status in a workplace, conveying that others are aware of contributions. At this level the contributor is credited with playing a meaningful role in pursuing the workplace's mission. To appreciate someone is to include that person in the tighter circle of colleagues with vested interests in moving their joint endeavor forward.

Accommodation goes still another step further by indicating colleagues' willingness to invest resources or even to inconvenience themselves to further one's work and increase one's sense of belonging. Accommodation also conveys an implicit valuing of diversity, in its recognition that all people are not the same. People have unique needs, aspirations, or preferences that they look to their workplaces to accommodate.

On the flip side of accommodation and feelings of belonging, there can also be incivility within the work community. Incivility encompasses a wide range of low-intensity negative social encounters. People convey incivility through words, gestures, facial expressions, and how they arrange themselves in space relative to one another. Workers participating in uncivil encounters are not only conveying unpleasant messages to one another, they are also performing for others in the vicinity who are observing the encounter.

Incivility has, as well, a quality of ambiguous intent. Ambiguity means that people receiving or observing a comment, or a scowl, may not know whether the person intended to offend. For example, people may walk by without responding to a greeting: Was that an intentional snub or did they just not hear or notice the greeting? The fact that they were not even *aware* of the other person's greeting misses one of the foundations of civility but does not necessarily signal that they meant to offend.

An offensive action or remark may be fully intended, however, to insult another person and to convey to others in the room that the other person is unworthy of their respect. But rather than making this point through shouting, profanity, and belligerent actions, the point is made with more subtlety. It may be that a workplace culture appreciates cutting wit over blatant acrimony but still does not give a high priority to maintaining civil discourse. Or it may be that the speakers want to slip insults under the radar of respectful workplace policies. Words and actions that look identical can reflect decidedly different intentions. That ambiguity raises serious challenges because intentions color the message. Regardless of the rationale, low-key insults can still pack a lot of power.

Beyond incivility, negative social interactions can become even more intimidating, hurtful, and even threatening. People may do things that are annoying and disruptive to others, such as talking loudly when others are trying to concentrate. Sometimes people may actually engage in abusive behavior or bullying—all of which require action by management. As an example of negative social interactions, one employee stated on a survey, "I personally don't get bullied, but I do see others getting bullied. People don't necessarily speak nicely to each other here. Also, people tend not to make eye contact around here; therefore, they don't have to acknowledge you. I think that's rude, too—to have your existence ignored is very disheartening, especially for people with low self-esteem."

To lay a basic foundation for promoting respect, workplace policies can be drawn up to address extreme behavior. It may not be possible or even advisable to outlaw sarcasm, but workplaces have a moral and a legal obligation to respond definitively to intentional intimidation, aggression, and violence. Such policies also allow civility initiatives to function by establishing a separate process to address extreme behavior that falls beyond the scope of work group processes.

Managing Workplace Civility

A positive social culture isn't the outcome of good intentions and cheerful slogans, any more than posting notices on walls proclaiming work spaces to be respectful will suffice to change behavior. Neither is there a shred of evidence in most organizations that require employees to take online training that completed modules on civility have any impact. When workplaces emphasize such tactics the result is often cynicism, as workers conclude that their employer's sole interest is in limiting exposure to legal liabilities: having "trained" the staff, they absolve themselves of responsibility for workplace dysfunction. To the extent that is true, leadership is abdicating responsibility for a key dimension of worklife. In addition to the immediate distress it causes, incivility can lead to lasting employee bitterness and distrust, and cause more workers to slide into the disengaged or burnout profiles.

For most employees, their direct supervisor functions as their point of contact with management. What happens in those encounters puts to the test how aligned an organization's espoused values are with its values in action.[2] For management those encounters are the channel through which people reveal if they are actively engaged with the workplace. These encounters have some performative qualities. Managers often receive training on supervisory communication upon which they may draw, and employees often guard their words and actions when encountering authority figures. But with experience, people gain a certain proficiency in seeing through artifice. It is possible to see beyond words to see what really matters in the workplace and to weigh this perspective against official value statements.

First-line managers have a central and ongoing role in the matches or mismatches that employees develop with their work. These supervisory relationships have the capacity to either alleviate or aggravate employees' susceptibility to experiencing burnout. Supervisors, in addition to their role in determining employees' workloads, serve a symbolic role in modeling behavior. Employees are quick to notice, for example, whether their bosses take time off or regularly work excessive hours. Social exchanges provide an important medium through which this influence occurs. In one study, for example, employees reported more incivility from supervisors who were experiencing burnout.[3] In another, employees reported greater feelings of efficacy from supervisors who were highly engaged in their work.[4] Still another piece of research showed that the quality of social exchanges between supervisors and employees boosted the extent to which employees' level of depersonalization modeled supervisors' level of depersonalization.[5]

Encounters among colleagues also convey information about the workplace culture and often prompt reciprocity. Other things being equal, people respond to respect with respect, and to disrespect with disrespect. In our research, we have found that worker incivility correlates more strongly with coworker incivility than with supervisor incivility.[6] By responding in kind to colleagues, people actively participate in the workplace culture. Although incivility among colleagues undermines trust and cooperation, giving back what you get affirms membership in the group.

Based on the survey data, we found interesting correlations between civility and the aforementioned profiles. The figure below roughly indicates the frequency of civil and uncivil exchanges experienced by people in each profile group. As shown, people in the

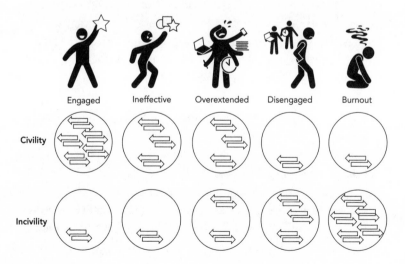

engaged profile both give and receive a great deal of civility. For those in the ineffective and overextended profiles, civil exchanges occur less often. For those in the disengaged and burnout profiles, civility occurs rarely. Turning to incivility, the engaged and ineffective profiles rarely experience negative encounters, but these seem to be a regular part of life for those in the burnout profile. Those in the overextended profile have uncivil encounters with supervisors a bit more often, usually concerning workload issues. People in the disengaged profile both give and receive incivility fairly often.

There is an important difference between the engaged and ineffective profiles: people in the ineffective profile have an average level of civility while those in the engaged profile experience frequent civility. The engaged profile is the only one that reaches near the top of the scale on civility, and it does so reciprocally, with people reporting that they both initiate and receive pleasant exchanges. In contrast, the engaged and ineffective profiles have nearly the same low frequency of incivility. Remember, civility includes expressions of appreciation, trust, and confidence in others. It not only fulfills a sense of belonging, but also contributes to a sense of efficacy and promotes autonomy. In a reciprocal fashion, receiving such messages runs parallel with providing that sort of encouragement to others. The striking difference between the engaged and ineffective profiles is a difference between a vibrant social dynamic for the engaged and a so-so social dynamic for the ineffective profile.

People in the overextended profile are closer to the midline on most measures. As noted previously, many people in this profile have one overriding concern: unmanageable workload that exceeds their capacity to recover. They are contending with relatively few problematic relationships with others, but they also lack the time or energy to participate in actively civil encounters.

In contrast, those in the disengaged profile have civil encounters very infrequently. People surveyed in this profile readily acknowledged that they did not initiate many civil exchanges with others.

Likewise, they reported fairly high levels of incivility, both as received from coworkers and supervisors and as initiated by themselves. Reciprocity is evident in both their low frequencies of civility and their high levels of incivility. Meanwhile, the social dynamics of the burnout profile differ from those of the disengaged profile by being even more intensely negative regarding incivility, both initiated and received.

In our work on improving workplace civility, we've found that problems grow out of inadequate expressions of civility as much as from excessive expressions of incivility. It makes sense that a higher ratio of incivility to civility pushes people toward burnout and away from engagement. It also makes sense that feeling exhausted and cynical while lacking a sense of efficacy interferes with one's capacity to engage in productive and fulfilling social encounters with other people at work. The causality works in a circular manner, with social encounters influencing how people feel, and feelings influencing how people interact with one another. A practical idea is to test the effectiveness of ways to improve the ratio of civility over incivility and, for the ways that prove successful, assess their downstream impact on burnout. Research on an organizational intervention approach called Civility, Respect, and Engagement with Work (CREW) demonstrated these effects. In a healthcare organization where some units had been working to achieve better job-person matches and avoid burnout, this process first increased the rate of civil encounters among people in those units. This alteration in turn was linked to a decline in rates of burnout, less disrespect, and greater trust.[7] And testing again, many months later, showed that this positive impact persisted.[8]

For any organization interested in preventing and alleviating burnout, a good place to focus first is on reducing incivility. After all, from both an employee and a workplace perspective, there's nothing to lose. This makes it an easier decision than, say, reducing workload, which some might object could cause a dip in productivity.

It is easier, too, than revising decision-making processes to be more participative, in an organization that values quick decisions under pressure. Compared to these other angles of attack, the idea of improving the ratio of civil encounters over uncivil encounters seems hard to oppose. Disrespectful behavior has no benefits at work. And improving civility and respect in workplace cultures has a real benefit in itself, even beyond the impact on burnout. It is all upside opportunity and no downside risk.

In Chapter 11, we will describe an approach we have found effective in improving civility in the workplace. This process builds on the understanding of burnout as a relationship problem, which develops through people's encounters with each other at work. For now, let us just say that, rather than sending offenders off-site to be repaired, this solution works by addressing relationships in the place where the problems exist.

Social Support

In our work on improving workplace civility, we have observed that even occasional rude encounters can matter greatly, whether they occur against a background of a socially supportive workplace culture or in a low-contact culture with few encounters among team members. In the latter situation, the rude encounter has a harsher impact, causing employees to ruminate over the incident, trying to understand its intent while wondering how they could have responded more effectively. In a weak workplace culture, people lack a foundation for hoping that things will get better.

In contrast, in an actively supportive workplace culture, people have a more solid foundation for responding constructively to rude encounters. They can count on the background of respectful encounters to see them through. They can see unpleasant encounters as a colleague slipping up temporarily, losing their cool, and likely regretting their nasty words. That greater confidence opens possibilities for constructive encounters in subsequent meetings. Furthermore, civil and supportive social encounters that convey appreciation, respect, and inclusion run contrary to cynicism, while bolstering feelings of efficacy. Social interactions with others confirm not only a sense of belonging but a sense of efficacy, as well. Even when people feel confident of their capacity to do excellent work, they gain something when other people acknowledge their adept contribution to the job. Supportive workplace cultures increase the chances of that sort of confirmation and reduce risks of encounters that undermine confidence. Essentially, workplace cultures with explicitly supportive social encounters actively draw people into more active, constructive relationships with their work. As one worker told us, "The culture and team I work in is wonderful. We're a highly collaborative, respectful, and fun team. I enjoy coming to work each day."

So how should a workplace improve the quality of social relationships and behavior? Acknowledging the social dimensions of mismatches opens strategies for taking action. A first step toward shared social solutions is establishing sufficient psychological safety to have the conversation. Without trust that a supervisor is approaching the conversation with the employees' best interests at heart, no conversation is going to happen. In many cases, employees report that in their prior years of education or training or job preparation, they did have sources of social support—friendly parties such as teachers, advisers, trainers, and mentors from whom they would receive important instruction, feedback, and guidance. Once they were employed in a regular job, however, they no longer had access to those people. Many of them say they miss that kind of support.

Indeed, when asked about what they thought would be the best thing to help them avoid burnout, the overwhelming majority said that it would be a similar source of social support—one or more persons whom they could trust as a confidential confidante and to whom they could turn for advice or help when they needed it. As

we shall see in chapters to come, the provision of this kind of social support by more senior or experienced colleagues is one of the
hallmarks of a culture of fairness and values. There are many ways
that social support can be enhanced within a workplace community,
including peer support groups, constructive feedback and performance evaluations, community-based activities for developing new
skills, counseling services, and more.

A healthcare team in a medical clinic shared an amazing story
of social support in their workplace. At the beginning of their shift,
the team would always have a short huddle in which they reviewed
the tasks for the day and the status of their patients, and then they
planned their course of action. The senior physician did most of the
talking, decided on work assignments, and made sure that everyone knew what they had to do.

One day, toward the end of the huddle, one of the more junior
nurses (who had never spoken up before) said that she was extremely worried because her child was very sick, and she had only
been able to arrange for childcare for part of the day—and she asked
if there was any way she could leave early to go home. The nurse
was anxious and even frightened about doing this, but she was desperate to figure out how to take care of her child. Other people on
the team immediately jumped in, however, with expressions of understanding and support, and suggested some alternative solutions
for how they could cover for the nurse that day.

It turned out to be a good one-time fix, but the event also had a
long-term ripple effect—it opened up the team process to be more
open and respectful and trusting. The huddle started to include a
quick check of how all the team members were doing each day and
if certain adjustments needed to be made. That meant that everyone started to talk a little more, and then they became less afraid of
raising a potential issue, such as a concern about a particular patient's progress. And that meant that everyone began to get to know
each other better and to develop more mutual trust. The sense of

community among the team members improved so much that they began to nickname their daily huddle the "cuddle-huddle." The "cuddle" addition was a small change—it had positive consequences but did not cost money or take much time—and the team had the control to modify their daily practice of the huddle. They collaborated with each other, they customized not only the huddle process itself but how they handled the rest of their team responsibilities, and they made the commitment to keep doing this regularly rather than only occasionally. This team was extremely proud and happy about their cuddle-huddle and willing to share their new wisdom with other teams, as well.

Another excellent example of creating social support came to us after one of our public talks about burnout. We were contacted by a screenwriter who was interested in how our recommendations about the importance of social relationships and community could be implemented with people who worked alone at home and did not know potential colleagues. (Note that this was a concern even prior to the pandemic.) Although screenwriters did belong to a union, they never got to meet or know each other unless they met on the picket line during a rare strike. Our general recommendation was to start small, beginning with a few other screenwriters who had similar concerns about being socially isolated. And here is what happened:

> I had an in-depth discussion about the topic and your insights with my "screenwriter captain" within the union. He thought the ideas were very interesting—especially about trying to build small pods where people really get to know each other on a more personal level. The challenge from his side was that restrictive rules within the union made it hard for him to exclude people in an attempt to form a small group. Still, he figured if he put out an open call to all the screenwriters to whom he's captain, the response would be relatively small. So

he put out that call for a team zoom meeting toward the end of February. It turned out he was right, and when we held the first zoom call, it was him and a staff member of the union, plus eight others (including me) for a total of ten people. A perfect number for everyone to talk about who they are and what they've been experiencing as screenwriters during the pandemic. There was a warm camaraderie although everyone was a bit shy. A month or so later he scheduled a second zoom call. This one was arranged around a topic of concern to all screenwriters ("producers making you do free work"). A few more people responded, but when it came time for the call there were a bunch of cancellations, and it was the *exact same eight people* who joined! You could already feel us beginning to cohere as a group with folks being more open in sharing their thoughts and frustrations. Toward the end of the meeting (thinking about what you had said regarding reward and recognition, and positive ways to build extra warmth and safety in these pods), I shared with the group the news that our captain's new movie was opening in theaters *right now.* The others picked up on this celebratory joy for him and shared it in a totally sincere way that only screenwriters who *truly* know the difficulty of that accomplishment could express. Seeing him light up with all that positive energy—and seeing all the good feelings and connection flowing among everyone who was expressing joy for him—was really magical. All at once everyone began expressing how much they valued coming together for these team meetings and hoped we could have more. It was so gratifying to behold—like planting seeds of something organic and watching sudden, unexpected blossoms.

A critical dimension of both these solutions—the screenwriters' and the healthcare team's—was that they developed in response to workers' direct input. These changes were made without disrupting normal workflow and put into practice with an established intention. The healthcare team discovered some new values that they could incorporate into their daily prep meetings. The individual screenwriters discovered a way to connect with other like souls to establish a beneficial social community. Both solutions developed a *customized* way of working together—a cuddle-huddle or a social pod—that met the present situation. There was not a solution "off the shelf" that would have had the proper impact. People needed to work together to develop a supportive social community.

Through their words, gestures, and actions during brief encounters or long conversations, people discover the extent to which they inhabit an inclusive workplace community or a fragmented collection of people. Some encounters can be especially fraught, such as when one is on the receiving end of important decisions regarding opportunities, recognition, or promotions (as the following chapter, on fairness, explores). People experience fairness not only through a decision's outcome and the decision-making process, but through the way decision-makers treat others during the process of coming to that decision.[9]

8

Fairness

Fairness is a relationship issue. Where it exists, it stands as evidence of respect and trustworthiness, two of the basic qualities of viable relationships. At work, fairness is perceived as the extent to which decisions are just and equitable. When an employer shows someone fair treatment, it confirms that person's full membership within the workplace community. In turn, people treat workplaces fairly when they respect their policies and procedures. A mutual commitment to fairness provides the necessary foundation to support engaged work experiences. People in a setting of fairness can realize their potential to work cooperatively in a shared mission.

It's no wonder that people lose trust in an organization that acts without fairness. Doing so implies that those in authority are not honest and do not respect employees for their contributions. These issues may be most evident during the evaluation and promotion processes, but day-to-day interactions can also be unfair—when there is inequity of workload or pay, or when people bend the rules or cheat to get ahead, or when people get blamed for things they did not do. If procedures for grievance or dispute resolution don't allow affected parties to have a voice, those procedures will also be judged as unfair. At a larger level, organizational policies that send the message that profits take precedence over employee well-being cause erosion of mutual respect and shared values. Cynicism, anger, and hostility are likely to arise when people feel they are not being treated with the fairness that comes from being treated with respect.

Respect and Reciprocity

As we saw in Chapter 7, mutual respect among all levels of employees is an essential condition for a viable, well-functioning community within the workplace. Respect is something not only felt by people but conveyed through actions. These actions can include both what people do that expresses respect, but also what they fail to do. The absence of appropriate actions (such as greeting someone with a smile and hello, or expressing thanks for some assistance) is often experienced as disrespect because of the lack of personal acknowledgment—it is as though that particular employee did not exist as a member of the workplace. And it is not just about words—nonverbal behaviors can also express powerful messages of respect or disrespect. For example, as part of research on civility in hospital settings, we asked nurses about coworkers' social behaviors they experienced as either positive or negative. There was strong consensus on what behavior was worst—in the phrase we heard repeatedly, it was others "rolling their eyes at me!" That particular reaction, whether silent or paired with sarcastic words, was always interpreted as a hostile put-down. It is a small, quick gesture of disrespect, rudeness, incivility, but it speaks volumes and carries heavy, negative weight. Indeed, the nurses considered it worthy of punishment: "There has to be a rule! Nobody should be able to roll their eyes and get away with it!"[1]

Relationships between people always involve ongoing exchanges, back-and-forth behaviors that can move in a more positive direction as people get to know each other and work together—or spiral downward into increasingly mean-spirited interactions. This continuous mutuality, of give and take, of tit for tat, can build greater respect and support, but it also has the power to make things worse—as when one eye-roll or insulting comment is returned with another.

If a relationship is going to become more positive and respectful, then the interpersonal dynamic has to be one of reciprocity. The exchange must create mutual benefit. This ideal has been enshrined in the Golden Rule—"Do unto others as you would have them do unto you." It has been restated in the ethical systems of virtually every culture and religion for centuries, in similar terms (as in "Love your neighbor as yourself," and "Never impose on others what you would not choose for yourself"). It is one of the most important moral principles for all people. For that principle to flourish, however, it has to be embedded in a culture of fairness, where there are both formal operating procedures and informal, everyday norms to enforce it. It relies on the social habits of working to understand what is happening to people besides oneself, to listen to them, and to respond with consideration and compassion.

There are many examples of reciprocity within a workplace culture. One involves the sense of a balance between what is given and what is received. If someone puts in a lot of effort to complete a task successfully, then that person expects to receive some positive return (such as acknowledgment, praise, a better task next time, and so on—and eventually better pay or promotion). If that reciprocal balance can be trusted to occur on a regular basis, it will promote better work in the long run. As many managers know, if you work hard for your people, they will work hard for you.

Another kind of reciprocity involves some sort of equal turn-taking—in which there is a regular rotation of who takes on some particular responsibility. This can vary from who takes the lead on a team presentation to who cleans up the staff refrigerator or brings the snacks for the Friday meeting. The basic point is that everyone pitches in and contributes to making things work well for the group—and the work is distributed fairly, so that no one person is overburdened or stuck with an unpopular task.

A different kind of reciprocity does not involve an exchange per se but underlies another process by which people give and receive—and that involves "paying forward" rather than "paying back." This kind of reciprocity is the basis for much of charitable giving in which one person helps or encourages another person who could benefit from that assistance. All of us have been helped by many people during our lives, and sometimes we can return the favor directly, or at least thank the person who made a difference for us. In some instances, however, we are not in a position to provide help of equal impact, or even to know who actually rendered assistance. But we can always choose to honor the act by helping other people when we see a need we can satisfy.

"Paying it forward" in the workplace can take many forms, but it is perhaps best demonstrated by mentoring—in which one person provides advice and guidance and support to another. In the workplace a mentor is often a more experienced and trusted colleague to whom other people will turn when they need some help and advice or have questions or worries about the job. This role is usually an informal one (largely because of the trust issue), but it can be of critical importance to many employees. Indeed, when we have asked workers to tell us what would help them most in terms of preventing burnout, the most common response is, "I wish I had someone I could talk to, safely and privately, whenever I have a problem or need some help." The absence of such a "safe haven" in many workplaces has led people to feel isolated and alone (even when they are surrounded by coworkers) and can exacerbate feelings of inefficacy, self-blame, and failure. Encouraging people to be mentors, and to give forward to younger colleagues the kind of help that older colleagues once gave to them, is an investment in a culture of fairness that can yield important social and moral dividends.

Equality and Equity

A common response to the question "What would be fair?" is a simple one: "If people were treated equally." Usually, this refers to what we consider to be commonly held privileges, like "equal rights" or "equal opportunity" or "equal pay for equal work" or "equal treatment under the law." Even if people differ in various ways, they are all entitled to the same human rights. At other times, however, the concept of equality means "everyone ends up getting the same." When people differ in the outcomes they enjoy—as when someone gets a "bigger slice of the pie" (or of the birthday cake) or gets more perks or accommodations while doing the same job—cries of "that's not fair!" tend to proliferate.

It is important to recognize that fairness is actually built on two core values—*equality* and *equity*. Equity means that people are treated without bias or favoritism. But equity recognizes that people have different conditions, which may need different actions to achieve equal outcomes. Both equality and equity are necessary for achieving fairness, but they follow different paths to that same goal. Equality is fair because it treats everyone in the same way, regardless of need. Equity is fair because it treats everyone differently, dependent on need.

It is critical to distinguish between resources and assets on the one hand and outcomes and results on the other, especially when talking about equality and equity. For example, consider the argument that to be fair to everyone, it is necessary to treat them equally. In some cases that may be true, but not in others. For example, if everyone received a pay raise that was an equal percentage of their salary, a richer person would receive a much bigger pay raise than a poorer person. Thus, an equal percentage does not lead to an equal outcome. If everyone has the equal opportunity to vote, however, then everyone has an equal outcome of casting their ballot—and that outcome is equitable, because of the absence of bias. This is why it is important to consider the distinction between equal inputs or "boundary conditions"—and equal outcomes. There may need to be different (unequal) steps taken to ensure truly equal outcomes for all.

Perhaps a very mundane example can make this point clear, one that has to do with the design of public restrooms. In large venues, such as theaters or sports stadiums, the restrooms for men and women often have an equal number of bathroom stalls—but the unequal outcome is, first, that many women stand in lines for a long time while many men are able to enter and exit reasonably quickly, and second, that women are more likely to miss the start of the second act or the next quarter. An equal outcome would be that everyone would be able to take care of necessary bodily functions in time. That would require an *equitable* approach of recognizing the different needs of women and men, and of providing more restrooms for the former than the latter, or perhaps more gender-neutral restrooms. Similarly, if there are differential boundary conditions affecting some groups of employees (prior experience, disabilities), then it is necessary to provide relevant and different (unequal) accommodations to ensure that everyone has the *equitable* outcome of *equal* chances for fair promotion.

The goal of equity is to guarantee a "level playing field" with no obstacles in anyone's way and where everyone has an equal chance of a fair start. Although the goal may be universally endorsed, the need for differential adjustments to ensure equal standing can still raise concerns about unfairness. For example, a benefit provided to workers with children, such as support for childcare, or work hours adjusted to school hours, may provoke irritation among workers without children, who feel that their own lifestyle needs are being ignored or disregarded. "Cafeteria" approaches to benefits can avoid this unnecessary social friction by presenting available choices and allowing everyone to construct sets of different benefits that are most relevant to their own needs. This is equity and equality working together to promote a culture of fairness.

We worked extensively with a division of a large institution that handled a variety of business and administrative services, including the maintenance of the buildings and grounds, business contracts, parking and transportation, mail delivery, and so on. Our research request was for a longitudinal project in which we could collect information from employees at two times, a year apart, so that we could begin to track changes in patterns of burnout and engagement over time.[2] The division agreed to institute an annual organizational survey of its one thousand staff members, which included measures of burnout (MBI), the six areas of work life (AWS), and other aspects of their experience. The survey was fully supported by the top management, who pledged that the overall results would be made public and would be used to help design interventions that would improve working conditions. A strategic planning group of staff from the various units was responsible for overseeing the survey process, for making sure that some of the survey questions focused on staff concerns, and for encouraging all staff to participate (anonymously and confidentially). The group's efforts were quite successful, as 87 percent of the employees participated in the first survey.

Before that first survey took place, we asked the senior administrators to predict what it might find. They predicted that two areas of work life would turn out to be most problematic: workload ("everybody always complains about working too hard") and reward ("everybody wants a pay raise"). It came as a major surprise when neither of those two areas stood out in the survey results. Instead, the employees named fairness as a major issue.

Setting aside his initial feelings of shock and disbelief, the CEO started talking with various groups of employees to discover why this was so. Many issues were raised by the staff, but the primary concern was the universally hated "distinguished service award," which included a monetary bonus. At first the CEO assumed that the amount of the award check might not be big enough, but we pointed out that the staff responses did not focus on the reward component, but instead on how unfair the award was. Staff viewed it as being rigged to go to the wrong people rather than to those who truly deserved it.

Why was the award considered so unfair? There were several reasons. Potential recipients had to be nominated by supervisors, but many supervisors considered this to be a waste of time and unimportant, so none of their employees were ever nominated. The award only went to one person, so the coworkers who had carried out a successful team effort did not get an award—only the leader did. If supervisors could not get a pay raise for a particular employee, they would say, "Don't worry, I'll get you the distinguished service award instead," even though that employee had not done anything to justify such recognition. And so on. In fact, when one of us discussed these first survey findings with the staff and mentioned that the results showed that they all wanted "to put a stake through the heart of the distinguished service award," the response was a huge round of applause.

The clear message to the CEO was to "do something about this!" But he pointed out, wisely, that he was not the right person to take on this task, as he had not understood what the problem was. Instead, he set up a staff team from the various units to assess what was not working right, and then to design a better process for rewarding employees who had done something special. It took a lot of time and effort to come up with a reward process that matched the specific characteristics of this complex organization, but finally the team presented a proposal that was adopted by the division.

After this change was implemented, the evaluation of fairness shifted from a negative one to a positive one on the second annual survey. A more significant outcome was the fact that the change resulted in a lot of optimism and hope: "If we were able to fix that problem, then we should be able to fix this other one!" The employees now felt very positive about their ability to collaborate with each other on shared issues, to design a customized solution for their particular workplace, and to commit to working on the task until there was a successful resolution. The organization decided to make the annual survey a permanent part of their continual self-improvement, and so it has become a regular "organizational checkup" that leads to regular projects to improve the workplace.

As a sidenote, we discovered another significant outcome from our partnership with this organization. We had a procedure for aggregating all of the employee responses within each department, so that we could provide a summary report for each unit (in addition to the overall report for the entire organization). One department in particular, Department D, had a very negative profile on the first survey, with a higher rate of burnout and more workplace mismatches (especially on fairness). Due to this response, just before the second survey, we inquired about what had been going on in Department D since the past year's survey. There was a long pause, and then a question: "How did you know?" It turned out that this department had experienced a crisis during the year, when several employees had been caught stealing organizational supplies and were subsequently dismissed. This raises the possibility that the negative pattern for the department provided a relevant clue that it was in trouble and not functioning well, and that an earlier intervention might have lessened or forestalled the subsequent crisis. It may be that such unit assessments are more useful than individual ones for managing job burnout, not only because they more clearly match the scope of managerial authority, but because they provide some important contextual information.[3]

The following story from a different workplace showcases the importance of eliminating favoritism and outlines how to pivot to fairness in the company culture. A small group within senior and middle management at a large insurance firm controlled the resources of the organization and doled out raises, promotions, and project funding to members of their clique. They overlooked excellent performance and dedicated service by people outside their immediate circle. Although other management problems were identified in the organizational survey, this issue of "loyalty awards" dominated the written comments and was clearly the strongest theme throughout the company.

Senior management supported a staff recommendation to establish a task force to review the organization's procedures for allocating significant rewards. The task force focused on two changes. First, the promotion procedures were made visible and inclusive. All promotion opportunities were announced publicly, including a description of the position along with the required skills, credentials, and experience. Previously, these decisions were made solely by the individual to whom the position reported. As a result of the more open promotion procedure, complaints about favoritism began to diminish. Second, the achievements of people working throughout the firm were highlighted. The company established a series of mini-awards for significant contributions and innovations throughout the year. The system prompted supervisors and managers to publicize the accomplishments of their own subordinates, because doing so enhanced the reputation of their units. Implementing this award system made senior management more aware of the specific contributions of all employees within the firm.

Several consistent themes emerge from these stories. First, both feature collaboration of many employees to solve a problem. Not only was everyone able to voice their point of view in a safe way, but many of them were then given the opportunity to work together to develop some better alternatives. This strengthened employees' sense of belongingness in their work community, as well as their sense of autonomy, competence, and efficacy in helping to actually make things better. In all cases, the focus settled on a positive goal, whether it was a smaller one (fix an award process) or a larger one (change practices to prevent favoritism).

In both examples it took a lot of combined effort to achieve a positive improvement in fairness, and it required everyone to commit to sticking with the process until a better outcome was finally reached. In all cases, people realized that while it was much easier to criticize and point out what was wrong than to redesign something that could turn out to be right, it was worth the journey. They recognized past flaws and made deliberate efforts to improve upon those in ways that fit their company culture. These two team processes were not as simple or straightforward as most people had expected. It took time, effort, communication, and trust to finally unite around a meaningful way for fairness to become a true organizational value and practice. One of the positive returns on this investment in commitment and collaboration was that many employees got to know each other better during this special team task. They then began to develop some friendships and socialize together, both in and outside of the workplace, which contributed to a better sense of community and social support.

We have often found that these kinds of moral mismatches (fairness and values) are not the first ones that people think about when it comes to the question of "How can we do things better here?" Workload and rewards are the more common focus. So, if they are not the first mismatches that come to mind, how do we even recognize and acknowledge problems with fairness and values? One of the advantages of the six areas of work life (AWS) questions is that they put these issues on the table. Survey responders evaluate if there are fair procedures for everyone and an absence of favoritism, and if there is consistency between personal and organizational values, and a commitment to quality.

Once these moral issues get raised, how do we even begin to think about them, and consider what it might take to improve "equality" or develop more "trust"? Is it possible to make a constructive difference on the moral dimension that can have a positive impact on many employees, rather than just a few? Yes, it is possible, as we will see in the next chapter.

9

Values

Values are what we consider right and wrong. They lie at the heart of whatever we do in life, and why we do it. The personal values that workers bring to the workplace often reflect a combination of individual commitments and professional obligations to which people align themselves by entering an occupation. Professional ethics, performance standards, and dedication to ideals combine to shape specific goals and bring cherished qualities to the way people do their work.

Values are often the motivating connection between the person and the job, which goes beyond the utilitarian exchange of time for money or advancement. Therefore, when there is a mismatch in moral values between worker and workplace, it can be one of the most critical factors in a person's experience of burnout. Time and again, we have seen examples where there may be an acceptable match on the social and capability dimensions for employees, but a bad fit on fairness or values undercuts that. In fact, a values mismatch is often a deal-killer, leading people to withdraw from doing their work well or to quit their jobs altogether. The significance of this moral dimension is not always well recognized or understood, especially in comparison to the attention given to the number of job tasks or the amount of salary. But workers are concerned about whether they are being treated fairly and whether they are doing meaningful work that they can be proud of.

When we assess the job-person match along the values dimension, our key question asks survey respondents to rate their agreement with a simple statement: "My values and the organization's values are alike." As noted in Chapter 2, those in the engaged profile tend to give scores in the "agree" range; those in the burnout profile register responses on the "disagree" end of the spectrum. Recall that a match is always a relationship issue. It is not about one side being correct—the workplace or the worker. Rather, it is whether they align or are at odds on a given dimension.

Values are not only important to people's decisions to accept their jobs—they are critical to people's staying with those employers. Most people do not begin with their "dream job." They may not even have a preference for what kind of work they will do in the future. In many cases, they stumble upon something that opens up a new possibility for them, which they had not considered before, such as when a temporary summer job turns out to be something they pursue as a career path. The inherent value of doing good work, in which workers take some pride, and that makes a difference for others, is what inspires and engages people to do their best for a long time, in any kind of occupation. This is part of why the job-person match on values often matters more than any of the other five areas.

A young woman we know who had studied environmental issues in college decided to seek out job opportunities that would align with her "green" values, such as support for renewable energy and nature conservation. Several years later, when she attended an alumni reunion, she told her adviser that she was currently working as an environmental consultant. Yet, as she was being congratulated, she grimaced. "Actually, I am going to quit," she admitted. Really? But why? Was she suffering from work overload, or lack of control, or lousy office space, or a measly salary? "No," she answered, "that's all fine." Was it a matter of unpleasant coworkers, or unfair treatment? Again: "No, those are OK." So why was she leaving? "The problem is that my actual job is to advise clients on how to raze the environment in order to build huge malls or parking lots—and this goes against everything I stand for," she explained. "I just can't do this anymore; I need to find some other kind of work that I can truly believe in and be proud of."

There are several ways in which people can experience a values mismatch on the job. The worst cases may be when the worker perceives a gap between what is said and what is done. A common version of this is captured by the phrase "You don't practice what you preach"—a situation in which workers feel forced into acting in ways that do not align with the purpose of their job, like when healthcare workers are limited to spending only fifteen minutes per patient, potentially sacrificing the quality of their care of patients because they have to handle a greater quantity of them. In other workplace situations, employees find that they are required to do secondary tasks (often administrative) that take them away from their primary responsibilities. As a result, they have to make trade-offs between the work they are prepared and want to do (and value more highly) and the work they are being compelled to do. They then have to cut back on doing their primary jobs well (to accommodate the other tasks) or work overtime to get all the tasks done. Thus, the experience of values mismatches can drive all three dimensions of burnout—cynicism about the moral dilemmas, inefficacy for having to fall short on the job, and exhaustion from having to take on too much.

The relationship between the job and the person varies among employees, depending on the qualities and life experiences each worker brings to the workplace, and this is certainly the case with values. For some people, values are the ideals and motivations that originally attracted them to their jobs. They may have a passion for this particular kind of work, and a dedication to doing it well, and they want to work hard to achieve these intrinsic rewards. But if they run into a severe values conflict (as did the physician we met in Chapter 1), nothing else about the work situation is worth the price of continuing in that particular job.

On the other hand, people who have different motivations for taking a job—such as earning a good salary, or commuting to a convenient location—may be more willing to tolerate mismatches between individual and organizational values, because those other aspects of work-life are more important for them. For example, consider the values conflict facing the environmental consultant described above. That same conflict was experienced by one of her colleagues and best friends at that same workplace, who also had moral qualms about the kind of work she had to do. But this colleague had a different personal situation—she was married and was the mother of two small children. For her, the area of rewards (rather than values) was most critical for her job-person match. She prized her steady income, the employer's on-site childcare, and other pluses of working and living where she did. Despite her misgivings about the values mismatch in her work, she was willing to make a compromise to keep the job and its family-friendly benefits.

Such issues vary for different workers because of the different personal values they bring to the workplace. What one individual finds ethically troubling may not cause any concerns for another. Some people find ways to cope with values mismatches by adjusting their own values to be more aligned with job norms. For others, that kind of solution is an unacceptable compromise.

As an example, consider the different responses of two psychotherapists, each operating an independent, solo practice. To get paid for providing therapy to their patients, both had to deal directly with the relevant insurance company. A common challenge for the therapists was that they and the company did not always see eye to eye on what was needed to take good care of the patient—the company wanted fewer sessions, and the therapists wanted more. How did the therapists manage to get an agreement that the insurance

company would authorize the needed number of therapy sessions? Often, they had to "game the system" by portraying the patient as more seriously ill than was actually the case, or by making
other claims that would support additional sessions. This meant
the therapists had to lie—the lies might be little white ones, or
shading the truth, but they were lies nonetheless. One therapist felt
strongly that lying and cheating were wrong and immoral, so eventually this became the breaking point for his burnout. "I couldn't
keep doing this over and over again. I couldn't look at myself in
the mirror each morning." He switched to a job in a healthcare
institution, where he could focus only on working directly with
patients (while someone else took care of insurance and payment
issues). The second therapist, however, took a different approach to
coping with this moral dilemma by adjusting his values. "The well-
being of my patient is the most important thing—so if I have to lie
and game the system to get the number of therapy sessions that
my patient needs, then I'll do whatever it takes. No problem." In
other words, the ends justified the means—a more Machiavellian
view, to be sure, but one that placed the highest value on patient
care. Obviously, a better solution for everyone would be to design
an improved system for paying for the costs of health care so that
there would be clarity and trust on both sides, and gaming the
system would not be necessary.

Meaningfulness of Work

What we have learned, time and again, about the key importance
of values at work is this: Everyone wants to do a good job, no matter
what the job might be. They want to feel good about what they have
accomplished, and they want to feel that their work has contributed
to the common good of the larger community.

The concern that one's work can sometimes compromise one's resolve to do good in the world was reflected in a well-known part of

Google's corporate code of conduct: "Don't be evil." Interestingly, when the company reorganized under the new name Alphabet, it replaced that phrase with "Do the right thing." But it is still so much of a concern that hundreds of employees formed a union in 2021. Rather than focusing on traditional bargaining issues of pay and benefits, the Alphabet Workers Union aims to protect employees who publicly criticize the company's response to societal issues (including criminal justice reform, gender and racial inequities, and ethical problems raised by artificial intelligence technologies) from retaliation. "As a tech employee," one engineer explained, "it's a reasonable ask to ensure that this labor is being used for something positive that makes the world a better place."[1]

All of these valued goals and motivations rest on the *meaningfulness* of the work that workers do. This idea has been around for some time now, but the methods for achieving meaning have not been so clear. Lofty mission statements, posters on workplace walls, and energetic pep talks may be designed to inspire with the ideals they express, but there is not a lot of evidence of their actual effectiveness. All too many workers have had the experience of entering a job with high optimism that it will put them in a position to have substantial positive impact, but then they encounter the "reality shock" of a system that makes it difficult for them to do the meaningful work they envisioned. Their initial engagement is beaten down into burnout.

As a perfect example of this we would share the story of Julie, who taught history and literature to eighth graders in a public school and had a reputation as an outstanding teacher. Students loved her, parents called to get their child enrolled in her class, and the principal rated her as one of the best. Young and successful, Julie was expected to have a long and distinguished teaching career. But then she decided to quit. Her decision came as a shock to everyone; some of her colleagues cried when they heard the news. At one time, Julie had been completely dedicated to the job. She loved that it allowed her to do things she valued highly—to make a difference in the world, to have a positive impact on other people's lives. But now she didn't think the job was worth it. At one time she had brought enormous energy and commitment to her work, putting in long hours and agreeing to do all sorts of extras, above and beyond the call of duty. Now she was exhausted, just going through the motions and doing the bare minimum. At one time she had been deeply involved with her students, attentive to their progress and achievement in learning, sensitive to their individual needs. Now she was more negative and cynical about their motivation and skills. At one time she had been confident that her efforts would pay off, that the kids would get a better education and a better start on life because of what she and other teachers were able to accomplish. Now she questioned whether the students were really getting what they needed; she even worried that children were being damaged by their interactions with overworked teachers like herself. To Julie, trying to do good came at too high a price.[2]

Part of the challenge that Julie and many others faced was that there was a big gap, a disconnect, between their values-laden aspirations (which had motivated them to take their jobs) and the reality of their daily chores. They could not see how their everyday jobs (the short-term tasks) were meaningful enough to achieve their desired goals (the long-term objectives). Recent research has developed a new approach to understanding this disconnect, however— in part by analyzing how one very high-profile project managed to enhance the meaningfulness of work.

In the 1960s, President John F. Kennedy tasked the National Aeronautics and Space Administration (NASA) with a historic responsibility to land an astronaut on the Moon and bring him back safely to Earth. A detailed analysis of archival evidence from this period reveals that Kennedy's communication of this objective featured four "sense-giving" aspects that enabled NASA's employees and the many contractors they engaged to see stronger connections between their daily work and NASA's space exploration purpose. The master strokes here were to:

- Narrow the focus to one goal.
- Shift from an abstract description of the goal to a concrete one.
- Set up clear milestones to the goal.
- Give life to the idea by using persuasive language and rhetorical techniques.

The result of these steps was that Kennedy articulated a single goal in very concrete terms—"This nation should commit itself to achieving the goal, before this decade is out, of landing a man on the moon and returning him safely to earth." Three milestones on the path to this goal were established as sequential projects: Mercury, to put a person in Earth's orbit; Gemini, to perform docking in space; and Apollo, to build all remaining capabilities needed to land on the moon. Kennedy's speeches were designed to excite and inspire everyone to achieve this goal:

Why, some say, the moon? Why choose this as our goal? And they may well ask, why climb the highest mountain? Why, thirty-five years ago, fly the Atlantic? We choose to go to the moon ... because that goal will serve to organize and measure the best of our energies and skills, because that challenge is one that we are willing to accept, one we are unwilling to postpone ... space is there, and we're going to climb it, and the moon and planets are there, and new hopes for knowledge and peace are there.

The impact of these four special efforts at sense-making gave NASA employees a stronger connection between the specific content of their jobs and the ultimate goal. They no longer saw their

work as an isolated series of tasks, such as building electrical cir-
cuits or mopping the floors. As one janitor said when asked about
his job, "I'm helping to put a man on the moon!" The value-relevant
conclusions of this research analysis of the moon mission were as
follows:

- In a way, Kennedy positioned employees to experience
  greater meaningfulness from their work by changing the
  meaning of work.
- When day-to-day responsibilities are imbued with a deep
  sense of significance, individuals thrive and weather even
  the most daunting aspects of employment including challenging work, low wages, and stigmatized work.
- Leaders are architects who motivate employees most
  effectively when they provide a structural blueprint that
  maps the connections between employees' everyday work
  and the organization's ultimate aspirations.[3]

Trust and Integrity

A workplace where people are both productive and proud of what
they accomplish rests on a solid foundation of integrity and honesty.
Integrity involves a strong consistency in truth—between principles,
statements, and actions. It is this foundation that breeds trust—
between leaders and employees, between coworkers on a team, and
between workers and the customers, clients, or patients they serve.
As we saw earlier, trust is a key factor in achieving better matches
in many areas, including workload, control, community, and fairness. Trust is crucial for people experiencing a sense of autonomy
in their work, free of micromanagement. It is a foundational quality
of respectful working relationships and for the establishment of
fairness in workplace decisions. Importantly, trust is something
that people have to actively build through their interactions with
others. It doesn't develop automatically.

The importance of trust between colleagues and coworkers has been underscored by George Shultz, who served in several major leadership roles under several US presidents. On the occasion of his hundredth birthday in 2020, he had this to say: "Looking back, I'm struck that there is one lesson that I learned early and have relearned over and over for a century. Put simply: 'Trust is the coin of the realm.' When trust was in the room, whatever room that was—the family room, the schoolroom, the coach's room, the office room, the government room, or the military room—good things happened. When trust was not in the room, good things did not happen. Everything else is details."[4]

In workplace cultures of truth and integrity, where everyone can count on each other to do what they have said they will do, mutual trust thrives and in turn enables good work and good outcomes. Another way of saying that trust and integrity are critical is to cite that common business maxim "Deliver what you promise." In contrast, when the work culture or the leadership style is one of "moral flexibility," in which ideals are applied inconsistently and words cannot be trusted, it is difficult for people to work effectively together and to accomplish important goals.

Just as we saw in the areas of both fairness and community, better matches require reciprocal trust. In Chapter 11, we will see how a workplace civility project produced increased trust among one group of coworkers. As people on this team increased their rate and proportion of respectful, appreciative social encounters, they trusted one another more deeply. The broader lesson learned was that trust needs to be a two-way street. If people want their colleagues to trust them, they also have to demonstrate that they trust those coworkers.

There are strong returns to be gained from investments in mutual trust. In conditions of high trust, everyone is motivated to work hard and take on big challenges, and they are more willing to contribute to overall success by providing helpful feedback, anticipating potential problems, and devising innovative solutions. Trust is the embodiment of respect, which, as we have been saying throughout this book, is central to promoting more positive relationships between the person and the job, in all areas of work life.

Several years ago, we worked with an organization that was facing a major crisis in values. Most of the staff members in this rural hospital had started working there when it was a public-sector enterprise, supported by public funds. They had all observed and been affected by the changes that came when a private-sector health maintenance organization (HMO), as part of its expansion into the state, acquired the hospital. Although the HMO had put together a plan for a gradual migration to its operating model, this approach was abandoned when a significant financial crisis hit the parent corporation. Instead of transitioning slowly, the HMO had abruptly imposed new control systems, including tighter billing policies and mandated treatment protocols, on a reluctant and unwilling staff. It was in this environment that we surveyed staff.

It wasn't only the suddenness of the change that bothered employees, or the fact that management had reneged on a promised plan. Much more fundamentally, the long-term employees of the hospital felt the new HMO model was contrary to their values about health care and that it took away much of their professional autonomy. "Where is the concern for patient care?," we heard. "Why can't I carry out my practice in the way I think best, without all these frustrating obstacles and constraints? Believe me, this is not why I went into medicine. I used to love this work, and was proud of what I did, but now I'm burned out and hate this job." The practices imposed by the new management of the hospital reflected a totally different view of customer service, financial controls, and clinical leadership. A shift of this magnitude is difficult enough, even with a well-planned transition. It is a critical problem when the transition fails to address the inherent values conflict.

The survey and its overall summary of employee responses placed the issue of values front and center. Consequently, the hospital embarked on a thorough review of how its various groups defined the values most central to health care. How did their priorities differ on matters of responsiveness to individual needs, accessibility to care, attentiveness to the emotional needs of patients, professional autonomy, and cost control? Then it held a series of town hall meetings, focus groups, and unit-level discussions, and fielded additional employee surveys—all part of a values clarification process designed to arrive at common understandings.

The outcome was the gradual development of a new, hybrid values system for the hospital. It differed from the one that had guided the hospital in its public-sector form but was also distinct from the prevailing culture of the private HMO. The success of the intervention showed up in increasingly positive ratings in follow-up assessments and in a renewed commitment to the work of the hospital. This was, in other words, a successful, intentional effort to customize a solution to the needs and characteristics of a unique organization. Neither of the two original values systems was the "winner." Instead, a third model developed in-house proved to be the best values framework for moving forward. Two other aspects of this effort to improve a values mismatch deserve to be underscored. It involved an extensive collaboration with all employees to develop better options for a set of operating values. And it expressed a long-term commitment to keep working on this process until a clear, shared solution was achieved.

Improving the moral dimension of mismatch can be challenging, since issues of unfairness and values conflicts are often hidden and not recognized or discussed in public ways. They are rarely a part of the regular agenda. Further, people may not want to raise any such concerns for fear of reprisal—worries about getting in trouble, dismissed, or even fired. This has meant that mismatches in moral dilemmas (as compared to social or capability mismatches) are more likely to be viewed as permanent and unchanging and even untouchable. This is an area in which people tend to feel trapped and uncertain of what to do. The choice would seem to be "take it or leave it."

Consider the following example of a professional at a prestigious consulting firm. He was earning a high salary but had serious disagreements about the ethics of the firm's client relationship practices:

> After I pushed back a couple of times and said that what we were recommending wasn't right for the clients, my boss cranked up the pressure on me and assigned me to only the most difficult clients. At one point I said to my wife, "It might be good if I got hit by a bus. I don't want to die, but I'd like to be injured enough that I'd have to stop working for a while." She said, "That's it; you're getting out of there."[5]

In situations like this, the best answer is to quit one's job and find another with a better moral match. This was the solution for the consultant, who lined up some independent opportunities and then made his move. Quitting was also the eventual choice for the teacher and the emergency physician we mentioned earlier. Leaving a bad situation can certainly be a good solution for oneself. It does not fix problems that will continue to have a negative effect on others, however, such as unfair discrimination, favoritism, or the destructive impact of sexual harassment.

It is sometimes assumed that this moral dimension is really just the domain of the individual, rather than the context. Personal values are one's own, just as every "moral compass" is individually set. They may differ from one person to the next, and the issues can be very sensitive ones. What follows from this assumption is that values should be kept private—and that each worker must simply adjust to the job demands and policies that exist in the workplace. Those demands and policies can pose some serious values conflicts for people, however, resulting in negative outcomes. Efforts to recognize and contend with these conflicts can help prevent burnout and build engagement.

Across the six chapters that make up Part II of this book, we have considered six critical areas of the job-person relationship: workload, control, rewards, community, fairness, and values. Mismatches of people with their jobs along any of these crucial dimensions push people toward burnout. By the same token, good matches in any of these areas push people toward greater engagement with their work.

As we move to Part III our focus shifts to practical strategies for creating more positive matches between workers and the workplace. We will offer guiding principles that have relevance regardless of which work life area presents the biggest problem for any given job. Having a set of guiding principles matters because building a better work life is an ongoing project. Conditions develop within people, across their workplaces, and in the larger political and social environment. Work life calls for agility, creativity, and a commitment to working with others. The solutions do not exist independently of the process for addressing the problem.

PART III

The Management

10

Creating Better Matches

In Part I, we explored what we called "The Marathon," taking a deep dive into the characteristics of burnout shops and the harmful impacts they can have on the people who work in them. We learned that workers' experience of burnout says more about the workplace than about themselves—and that has important implications for defining problems and exploring solutions. To focus more on *who* is experiencing burnout than on *why* is akin to diagnosing the canary and trying to make it more resilient, rather than dealing with the coal mine's toxic fumes. The answer to *why* lies in the relationship between the worker and the workplace, and whether that relationship constitutes a good match or a bad fit.

We called Part II "The Mismatches" and devoted each of its six chapters to one area of the job-person relationship. Mismatches in *workload* and *control* compromise people's capability to complete job tasks effectively. Mismatches in *reward* and *community* produce a socially toxic environment in which it is difficult to work well with other people. Mismatches in *fairness* and *values* strip the workplace of its moral character, which undermines people's goal to do the right things in their jobs. But it is possible to pivot in these six areas away from the mismatch and toward a match. As we have seen in a variety of stories, mismatches can point to ways to improve difficult environments and guide organizations' work toward solutions.

And now we have reached Part III, "The Management," and are ready to learn what it takes to redesign a specific job environment to make its productivity more sustainable and gratifying for everyone who works there. The essential steps on this journey were outlined in Chapter 3. They will be discussed in much more detail in this chapter, on creating better matches, and Chapter 11, on making matches work. As we work toward change, it is not necessary to start from scratch to achieve better job-person matches in the workplace. There are lots of success stories out there, and we can follow them as examples. There are many options that can lead to improvements, so it is important to select and support those that have the greatest probability of success. These will be the ones that have received broad endorsement by managers and employees—usually because they collaborated significantly to arrive at them.

The Core C's of Change

Positive changes can involve any one or more of the six mismatches, they can involve small changes as well as large ones, they can vary in financial cost from none to a lot, and they can be done within smaller groups and units or at the larger scale of the whole organization. Regardless of the area or scope, we recommend an approach to problem-solving that combines the power of collaboration, customization, and commitment. These "three C's" all serve to boost participation and achieve lasting improvements in the life of the workplace.

To *collaborate* is to ask all employees to be part of making things better. Just as relationship problems between people cannot be resolved unilaterally, job-person mismatches at work are shared problems that require shared solutions. It does not work to send someone off to recover only to return that person to the same mismatch that generated the problem originally. It also does not work when human resource professionals devise a workplace health initiative, no matter how wonderful, and then spring it on an unsuspecting workforce. All affected people should have a role to play in the entire change process—from recognizing problems, to understanding problems, to generating solutions, to implementing solutions, to evaluating outcomes. For example, workplaces that addressed fairness mismatches (Chapter 8) relied primarily on making decisions more *collaborative.*

To *customize* is to adapt a proposed change to the local culture and type of occupation. It is obvious that there are no silver bullets, and no one "best practice" that fits all solutions. It is even difficult to pin down best practices, because mismatches and their resolutions are so distinctive to their situations. The unique qualities of the workplace and of the people who work there point toward creating matches that resonate with the local environment. A collaborative process can customize initiatives to fit the workplace culture, improving chances for success. For example, as we saw in Chapter 4, a workload match was created by designating times at which there would be no interruptions or visitors to the office—a solution that was suited to the conditions in that office but might not work in another organization.

To *commit* is to sustain the effort to make positive improvements. Mismatches may not resolve quickly, so solutions require a long-term commitment to making progress toward a better job-person relationship. It takes time to learn a new way of doing things, and to then adopt it and put it into regular practice. There will be glitches and bumps along the way, requiring further adjustments and course corrections. But if everyone recognizes the value of the desired goal, they will be more willing to keep trying to get it right. The example in Chapter 9 of addressing a value mismatch in a hospital called on everyone in the workplace to commit a lot of time and effort to developing a new hybrid value system that could accommodate them all.

Discovery of Better Matches

How can we improve the coal mine or the burnout shop? As we discussed earlier, there are many possibilities for better job-person matches in all the six areas. But the process—discovering those multiple options, choosing which ones to pursue, and how—is a path that includes three clear steps: first identify the area of a problem mismatch, then pivot to consider a range of positive matches, and, finally, pursue attainable goals.

IDENTIFY THE AREA OF A PROBLEM MISMATCH

Begin with finding some current mismatches that could be improved or fixed, then review the list and prune it down to just one mismatch. Why only one? As we will discuss a little later, when we talk about "attainable goals," it is wiser to start small, with one achievable goal, to maximize the possibility of achieving some success. After one win, you will be in a better position to move on to a second one. In larger organizations, however, the "one goal" might end up being different for some units than others, depending on the nature of the experienced mismatch. But "one at a time" is usually better than "doing it all at once." Nevertheless, it is helpful to begin by searching widely for several potential candidates for a mismatch fix.

There are many ways in which that search can take place, beginning with already available sources of information. Have certain topics come up in regularly scheduled meetings, such as with a supervisor or with team members? For example, are there recurring suggestions or complaints about workload (such as the number of working hours or lack of needed supplies and equipment), control (such as lack of flexibility in job assignments or in dealing with family emergencies), or rewards (such as lack of compensation for working overtime or taking on an extra assignment)? Problem mismatches along the community, fairness, or values dimensions may not get voiced as often, especially if they involve sensitive information, but these may surface in such meetings if some major difficulties or conflicts have occurred.

These types of regular meetings are a primary way to get input from larger numbers of rank-and-file employees—and input is critical in a collaborative search for identifying a good mismatch to fix. Not only do workers have direct experience with these chronic "pebbles in their shoes," they will have some good ideas about viable ways to solve the problem. Moreover, they need to be on board, with the choice of both the mismatch and its management, and thus to *commit* to making the improvement work—otherwise, the change will never happen.

Another available source of information comes from managers. The conversations they have with people in multiple units can provide continuous and timely comparative information about matches and mismatches. Some units may have more reports of unresolved conflict or complaints of excessive workload. Managers have deeper insight into the context in which incidents arise, allowing plans to be customized more closely to the situation.

In one organization, a survey of community issues provided mixed results for one unit that included elevated levels of both respect and disrespect. The unit manager was able to explain this apparent contradiction by describing a fragmented work group. Within cliques, encounters were respectful and appreciative; between cliques, interactions were disrespectful and lacked consideration. Based on this assessment, a strategy to improve this community mismatch was designed differently and customized to address this unique problem.

Institutional sources of available information regarding mismatches can also be found in larger organizations that regularly gather data on their people and products. This information can be especially useful when it can be organized by unit or work group because it helps to map where things are going well and where things are strained. When existing institutional data can be organized by the same framework that is used in an institutional survey, it can expose patterns of mismatches. For example, units with more people working overtime or taking sick leave may have more burnout profile or overextended profile workers, due to higher levels of exhaustion. Recall the story in Chapter 8 describing how a work unit that reported a big fairness mismatch was identified as a place that had major problems with cheating and theft.

Although multiple sources of information add depth, they must be integrated into a coherent model of the workplace. In large, complex workplaces, units can differ considerably on the problematic mismatches, as well as the intensity of their occurrence. An implicit advantage of this diversity is that work groups that are doing well may have structures or processes that could be identified as ways to achieve better matches. In other words, they could be successful models of what to do better, and their practices could then be adapted to units that are struggling with mismatches.

Sometimes it is not possible, however, to get sufficient mismatch information from standard sources. These sources may be limited or restricted or inaccessible. Or they may not exist at all. In this case, the first step involves finding new ways to find out what the problem mismatches might be. Usually, this means going out and asking people some systematic questions about their workplace experiences, via some sort of survey or interview.

If organizations are concerned about the well-being of their employees, they might undertake an organization-wide assessment, arranging for everyone to complete a validated set of surveys and then analyzing the responses and issuing a companywide report about what has been learned about potential mismatches, which could then be addressed. Sometimes such an assessment can be done in-house, if there are the necessary resources to carry it out.

Or it can be outsourced to a company that can perform the assessment and provide additional consultation.

The value of an organizational survey is that accurate assessments establish a shared understanding of the mismatches people are experiencing across the units within the workplace. It is a shared foundation for collaboration and opens possibilities for customizing the solution by clarifying the distinct features of prevalent mismatches. In this way it can make a powerful contribution to designing an initiative. In our own work, we have used a combination of two measures, the aforementioned MBI and the AWS, to assess the five work profiles and the six areas of mismatch.[1] But there are other surveys that can be used as well.

Not all workplaces have the capacity or willingness, however, to invest in this kind of organizational assessment. In this case, groups of workers may have to look after themselves and do a group assessment on their own. This type of informal reflection on how things are working out on their current job can provide insights into mismatches that are problematic, as well as into matches that are sources of strength and resilience. So how can this informal assessment be done? As it turns out, we have already done the work for you, as we developed an informal assessment that groups can do on their own.

In an earlier book we offered a set of questions designed to help people assess their own experiences in all six areas of job-person mismatch.[2] The Appendix to this book, "Assessing Your Own Relationship with Work," is an adapted version of those questions. This is not a validated test that can generate meaningful statistics; rather, it is an opinion survey. But it can stimulate some thinking within a group about what might be a mismatch that is worthy of a good fix. For each of the six areas, there are variable elements listed, such as "My opportunities to show initiative" (in the Control-related set) or "Appreciation from others" (in the Rewards-related set). Each statement should be rated as one of three options: Just Right (0) or

Some Mismatch (1) or Major Mismatch (2). Total scores for each area can range from 0 to 10, with higher scores indicating a more serious mismatch. The actual numbers do not matter that much. It is more about identifying areas where a lot of people are experiencing mismatches—and where they might be open to changes that would make a positive difference. The goal is to eventually identify a problem, a "pebble in the shoe" that many people agree they would like to be rid of.

PIVOT TO CONSIDER A RANGE OF POSITIVE MATCHES

Once a specific mismatch has been identified as a problem that needs solving, we move on to the next step: pivot to a more positive match. The negative elements of the mismatch often provide some clues as to what could be improved. For example, the office staff described in Chapter 4 had a workload problem—lots of tasks they could not finish on time. But in analyzing their situation, they realized that it was not a problem of unrealistic demands, or of insufficient training, or a lack of the necessary tools or needed information—all reasonable possibilities, but not in their case. Rather, the problem was the number of unexpected interruptions during their work hours—and this led them to consider possible ways of modifying their schedule so that they could have more quiet time and fewer distractions and more opportunities to get advice or consultation about a particular task. Thus, their "pivot" to a more positive match focused on a solution that was highly relevant and customized to their situation, and that was under their control and doable.

Having a model that focuses attention on six potential mismatches offers the important benefit of bringing a variety of new perspectives to what may seem like a standard "old" problem. For example, many *workload* mismatches might actually be better understood as involving issues of insufficient *control* or difficulties in the functional *community* of the team. The process of giving one employee a special award might appear to be a concern about *rewards,* but as we saw in Chapter 8, it might really be a dispute about *fairness.* Thus, the six areas of job-person match can provide multiple lenses for looking at the same problem and then identifying more viable solutions.

Furthermore, a critical part of a positive pivot is not only thinking about the goal of the desired match, but considering the relevant psychological needs underlying a better fit between the person and the job. For example, a community match might involve enhancing people's sense of *belonging* to the unit or team. Or it might promote their sense of *psychological safety* and *fairness* within the group, as would a match on fairness. *Meaning* will be important for a better match on values, and *positive emotions* will probably be critical for better matches on reward and recognition. The needs for *autonomy* and *competence* are likely to be especially relevant for matches on control and workload.

Usually, there are many possibilities for a better match, and it is critical to consider as many of them as possible. These can range from the obvious (fixing or upgrading dysfunctional equipment) to the innovative (redesigning patient-intake procedures). Some options might be more feasible than others in terms of how easy they would be to implement or how much they might cost. Some might involve bigger changes than others, and some might be more meaningful to people. Each option will have both pros and cons, and it is important to evaluate these carefully. This usually means getting a lot of input from many people—especially those who will be most affected by the change. It may not always be possible to get complete consensus on how best to achieve the desired match, but there needs to be enough of a shared commitment, to both the specific goal and the process for getting there, that everyone will be on board to take the necessary actions.

Essential to any pivot is to pose a basic question: What will success look like? In other words, if we go ahead with this process, how will our work life be improved? The change may take some time and effort to implement, so how will everyone know when they've gotten to a better place? Too often, we have seen organizational change efforts launched with a lot of bells and whistles and catchy slogans at the outset, but without having prepared people for what is to come, or explained why that outcome will be worth it. In some cases, the benefits of the new change are not equal for all employees; for example, a new financial system might make things better for one department, like accounting, by adding more workload to another team, like sales. Moreover, the answer to "What will success look like?" must be specific and unambiguous rather than vague. "Reducing burnout" is not a specific goal, but designing better matches can be. Changing the annual staff appreciation event to be a more meaningful form of recognition or changing the criteria for a special award to be more fair—goals such as these can be visualized in terms of what actual success will look like, and their accomplishment will help reduce the kinds of chronic mismatches that lead to burnout.

The basic challenge for any change effort, however, no matter how positive the goal, is that "things will get worse before they get better." This is a universal truth that needs to be explicitly recognized and prepared for. First, any change involves stopping or dismantling something that has existed before (and that can make things ambiguous and even scary). Second, the next step involves installing or teaching something new (and there will be confusion and glitches, and mistakes will be made). Third, the improved change finally will be fully implemented (but it will take both time and practice to make it a comfortable routine). Therefore, it is critical that the desired goal of a positive match must always be visible, clearly understood, and regularly assessed for progress, if it is going to motivate everyone to keep on going until the goal becomes reality.

BEGIN WITH ATTAINABLE GOALS

As stated earlier, it is better to start small, with a meaningful but doable goal, when trying to manage a mismatch. In other words, begin with the "low-hanging fruit." There are multiple reasons for this recommendation. First, any new initiative adds yet another demand to people's work lives—and when trying to appeal to an exhausted and frustrated community of workers, it is best to make that demand a modest one that does not add to their burden. Second, a smaller, achievable goal will have a greater likelihood of success, which can inspire people to try to fix something else. A few small steps in the right direction can be the beginning of something great. Third, doing one thing well is often better than trying to do too much all at once. It is not necessary to fix a lot of things simultaneously (and it is often not possible), so a clear focus on improving one thing that people really care about is a better strategy.

Getting relevant input from all the relevant people is essential to determining what would be a feasible and possible goal for them to pursue. Their knowledge and experience can point out in advance potential pitfalls, or erroneous judgments, about what it will take to make change happen. Moreover, their motivation to commit to improving a mismatch will be higher if they have a recognized role in shaping the process to achieve it and customizing it to fit their needs.

Any kind of improvement, no matter how wonderful it will be, usually involves some addition—of time, effort, and extra modifications. As we pointed out in Chapter 3, *additions* need to be balanced by *subtractions,* to avoid overload. What can be eliminated, or reduced, or redesigned to lessen the job burden? Some subtractions may be easy to identify, but others might require "breaking set" from routine thinking. An analogous example is the standard safety announcement on airplanes, which asks passengers to "find the nearest exit from the airplane" and advises that it might be behind them rather than in front. In a similar way, potential subtractions may exist but not always be fully visible, due to force of habit.

USE THE PROFILES TO GUIDE ACTION

A practical implication of the five profiles is that they point toward action. Workplaces cannot take action in all directions at the same time. They have only so much capacity to address issues arising from mismatches; they need to direct that action to where it will have the greatest impact. Further, people can become irritated with workplaces attempting to address problems that workers are not experiencing. People generally want to meet their work demands and exercise their expertise. For example, if they experience their work as intrinsically rewarding, they do not want to be interrupted by an online module on making work more rewarding. So, targeting action makes sense all around. It is important to identify the mismatches of greatest concern for each work group.

The burnout profile presents serious challenges because exhaustion, cynicism, and inefficacy have the potential to aggravate one another. When exhausted, people have less capacity to take on anything new, making them less open to change. Cynicism reduces their trust in the capacity or willingness of others to have their best interest at heart. Inefficacy reduces confidence in their own capacity to overcome challenges. The three dimensions build on one another in ways that perpetuate burnout. One of the challenges in well-intended efforts to alleviate burnout comes from the fact that people experiencing burnout are rarely open to change. They feel too exhausted to take on anything new. Even an initiative to help them be more rested can seem like too much work. Growing psychological and physical distance from colleagues has made them cynical, and that cynicism then prevents greater closeness. People experiencing burnout may be dubious about others' good intentions. For example, they may view suggestions to relinquish one area of their workload—participating in certain meetings—as attempts to marginalize their impact among their colleagues. Low efficacy also indicates low confidence in their own capacity to change their situation. From this perspective, the first step in alleviating a colleague's burnout is not trying to improve all six areas of work life but reducing workplace pressures to create opportunities to connect with that person, building confidence in the assistance as well as in themselves.

The overextended profile presents the most straightforward course of action. People in that profile have serious mismatches with workload. Actions to reduce work demands or to increase resources so that people can meet those demands will have meaningful impact. The necessary resources depend on the circumstances. For example, one can address *quantitative* workload problems, having to do with the number of tasks to be performed in a given time, by reducing that number of tasks. But *qualitative* workload problems may have more to do with the complexity or emotional demands of work and may call for building greater expertise or providing extra emotional support rather than reducing the number of demands. Still other approaches to workload mismatches are to improve work schedules and provide opportunities for recovery after periods of heavy work.

Those in the disengaged profile present a distinct set of challenges in that workload is not an issue for them—but everything else is. People in the disengaged profile may feel confident in their own capacity for action or change. They have the energy necessary to try something new. They will only expend that energy, however, if they have confidence that an initiative will be effective and in their personal interest. Their negative evaluations of everything except workload do not bode well for their receptivity to initiatives from management or from support services, such as training or human resources. They doubt the utility and the good intentions of such programs. Further, they have valid reasons to doubt such initiatives, given the history of workplaces implementing programs on well-being or leadership that lack rigorous evaluations on their efficacy. In any case, addressing workload will not have much of an impact with people in the disengaged profile. It is important instead to listen and respond in ways that build a trusting working relationship. People in the disengaged profile often have serious mismatches on values. Focusing on the values they want to bring to their work can open possibilities.

The ineffective profile calls for action that moves from okay to positive. People in this group are not dealing with many strains or problematic aspects of the workplace culture. But they are also not experiencing many positive or pleasant aspects of the job. In particular, they could benefit from improvements in the social realm, which would yield more encouragement, help, recognition, and sense of belonging to the workplace community.

The engaged profile also provides direction for action. Although one may simply feel relieved and move on to more pressing issues, it is necessary to provide ongoing support to good matches in relationships with work. Understanding what is working for people in the engaged profile can provide useful information for improving relationships with work for people in other profiles.

Redesign of Better Matches

Mismatches reflect poor design. Poor fit with a job is like sitting in a boxy, narrow chair. You cannot get comfortable. You have difficulty standing up. A poorly designed workday is like sitting through a play in desperate need of a director to pick up the pace and get to the point. When experiencing mismatches, people have difficulty establishing a flow (as described in Chapter 6). Work processes seem awkward, and it takes too long to accomplish anything. It follows that poor design leads to frustration and distress.

Mismatches occur when individuals and workplaces fail to resonate with one another. For example, essential to the design of an Eames office chair is the capacity for people to adjust it to fit their bodies, but the chair is only really comfortable if people do make those adjustments. Likewise, a well-paced drama is compelling only if people put away their cell phones and pay attention to the stage. The way people behave is an integral part of design. Good design doesn't just happen to people; good design arises from dialogue between people and their contexts.

In its early days, the US Air Force aspired to design the perfectly proportioned cockpit: because jets are so fast, pilots should be best positioned to respond instantly. The Air Force meant to design aircraft to fit the average-sized man, not simply in height and weight, but with average-sized forearms, feet, neck, and other bodily elements. After much effort, engineers discovered that no one was average on all their criteria simultaneously. In fact, few people were average on even a short list of the criteria. This realization led to abandoning the idea of the perfectly proportioned cockpit and aiming instead to make components adjustable, allowing people with a wide range of configurations to operate the aircraft comfortably and effectively. Excellent design is accommodating.

Exceptional design is intuitively obvious, or 99 percent invisible.[3] The processes of defining the problem and creating the solution have already occurred. For example, a door should not need a manual: the design of a first-rate door conveys, as one approaches it, whether to push, pull, or slide. Ideally, it would go without saying (or at least without a sign saying "push" or "pull"). Excellent design is intuitively obvious.

Outstanding design is not a one-time event but an ongoing process. Getting it right at the beginning does not mean clear sailing will follow. Excellent design reflects a vibrant, ongoing dialogue of people with their workspaces. Usually, the process of improving on design unfolds gradually, in small steps. Small improvements in day-to-day work life accrue over time to nudge things in the right direction. A slow-paced process fits well with addressing burnout, which can develop gradually and endure for a long time. Although there may be considerable urgency in addressing aspects of burnout, the impact of these actions will occur gradually. Although it is important to get something going, it is critical to bring people along with the process.

USE DESIGN GUIDELINES

The bottom line is that poorly designed work, which frustrates hopes and value commitments, is what burns people out. Can design principles help to create better connections with work? A good place to start is with three principles of design: balance, unity, and rhythm.

Maintaining *balance* is an issue for workplaces and people. Finding balance considers workplace structures and processes with regard to the core motives that people bring to work. What are the implications of this move for people to fulfill their sense of belonging, efficacy, or autonomy? What are the implications for their sense of fairness? Does this initiative make their work more meaningful or just add another layer of activity?

When planning interventions, a useful practice is envisioning ways in which these efforts can restore balance. One central balance is between demands and resources, including the critical resources of employees' time and energy. Sometimes people become overwhelmed by their workload because no one ever thought through the time demands. This sort of imbalance can be minimized through an analysis of the time required against the time available in the context of multiple demands at work.

Another perspective on balance is between the intensity of psychological motives and opportunities for addressing them. A work group integrating unfamiliar technology in their work may be starved for experiences that confirm their sense of competence and effectiveness. For example, a group accustomed to delivering their services person to person may lose some confidence when shifting to virtual service delivery. This happened often during the pandemic for many people, such as teachers in schools, who now had to master new technologies immediately, to work with their students online. A useful part of a support plan during such a transition includes building in occasions that confirm the quality of their learning and the long-term benefits of new skill sets to their career development.

Coherent values with a shared mission bring a sense of *unity* to the workplace, reflecting a clear set of principles and conduct that are evident in day-to-day activities. One sign of unity is that, despite the complexity of a large organization, employees can readily state the core principles of their workplace (as we saw in Chapter 9 in the NASA moon project example). A clear mission consolidates employees' range of activities into a coherent contribution. Taking a stand on a discrete set of values provides a focus, and it means that customers and employees encounter a consistent message whenever they interact with the workplace.

On the one hand, the optimal workplace culture is true to its established principles; on the other hand, the culture is open to new ideas. For instance, bankers closely follow existing protocols on tracking and reporting information while remaining up to date on new developments in their field. Having the best solution for today does not mean you have the best solution forever. A critical step for interventions intended to develop a coherent approach to multiple values is working through their inevitable contradictions. For example, tension can develop between providing cost-effective care and showing compassion. Solutions favoring cost-effectiveness put limits on the amount of time providers devote to each patient. This simple solution is easy to measure; however, it assumes a zero-sum game of money versus compassion. Research has demonstrated, on the contrary, that showing compassion toward patients saves money in downstream care.[4] Compassionate care is associated with patients reporting less pain and being more compliant with their treatment and medication regimen, both of which reduce costs while increasing patient satisfaction. Integrating these two values requires developing a unified vision across treatment providers and executives to assure the best use of providers' time.

Resolutions on this scale do not emerge effortlessly. They occur from the hard work of integrating different perspectives into a unified commitment to the workplace's core mission. The strategies explored in Chapter 9 (on the values mismatch) assist with fostering unity. A key quality of contemporary workplaces has become the capacity to maintain a core focus while embracing flexibility with a workforce that is diverse in many ways.

Rhythm brings in the dimension of time. The repetition of one workday following another establishes a rhythm, but one that becomes much more engaging with variety that emphasizes some days over others. The rhythm as people move through their workdays makes work more predictable; it brings comfort. Regularity can dull the mind, however, allowing people to settle into routine thinking rather than developing their creativity or responsiveness. Even Baroque music, despite its insistence on regular tempo, slows down to signal the end of a movement.

Although the familiar is cherished, the same old / same old gets old. Rhythm in work life combines periods of low intensity with periods of greater intensity. In a shoe store, intense periods with multiple customers vying for the attention of a few employees open opportunities to realize talents, with potential bonuses down the line. But few want to live that way throughout every workday. It can quickly become too much. Alternating intensity with periods of calm allows people to maintain their energy and involvement by defining some recovery during workdays, but it also supports their sense of efficacy by giving them moments to reflect on what they have accomplished.

As with a symphony, the elements of a complex workplace move at different speeds. The rhythm in the executive suite may depart greatly from what is happening on the shop floor or in the human resources department. And within those units, individuals will shift in the priority they give to their various pursuits. The emergency department has the opposite pace of post-operative care units. Although it is certainly possible to get everyone on the same page, it may not be possible to get everyone on the same page at the same time.

BUILD IN PROGRESS CHECKPOINTS

Up to now, we have discussed how to come up with better matches in one or more of the six job-person domains—identify a problem mismatch, pivot to consider positive alternatives, start with smaller and doable goals, and then focus on redesigning a better match. But wait, there's more! Not only is it critical to design a specific goal of a better match, but it is also essential to design a clear plan for tracking progress toward that goal. And given the inevitability of problems or glitches along the way, a plan for dealing with those must be prepared as well.

Estimate dates on a timeline. When will the change process begin, and when is the estimate of when it will be completed, and what might be some significant milestones, or feedback points, along the way? Setting up a map of the path to the goal of a better match, and sharing it widely—along with any needed adjustments to the pace or activities—will help everyone know what's going on, what they need to do to help, and when it will get done (are we there yet?). The design principle of rhythm can be particularly useful here.

- *Attend to the rhythm.* When rolling out a new program or determining where and when to provide additional support, it is important to attend to the rhythm of the various units across a workplace. Supports are not infinite. They require careful attention to assure they go where needed and are not dissipated on units at other points in the cycle of intensity. Even within units in need of support or ready for new programs, flexibility matters. Whether through surveys, talking with people, or watching how things unfold, a first step is attending to what is already going on. Attending closely allows innovation to fit into the work group's existing rhythm.
- *Make something special.* Emphasis defines a rhythm. To get with the program or to play the tune, people need to feel the downbeat. Putting extra emphasis on an initiative lets everyone know that this is the start of something new. Including signal events in the unfolding of an intervention helps to establish rhythm as well. They let people know the initiative to be outside of the usual mode of business.

Occasional landmark events pertaining to the initiative help to give it presence in the life of the work setting.

. *Maintain the rhythm.* Workplace initiatives need to endure. A solid design serves this goal by anticipating glitches, setbacks, accidents, and moments of inattention. A plan that predicts that all will go smoothly is not a complete plan. By clearly focusing on the objectives of improving the relationships of people with the workplace, work groups can find their way through problems along the way. Intervention plans benefit from anticipating potential hiccups going forward. These reassure people that minor crises have been anticipated and can provide some direction in responding effectively when they do occur.

Set a permanent agenda item. If it is important, it should be on the regular agenda—always, until it gets done, when the goal has been accomplished successfully. That is part of the rhythm too—there will always be a regular, normal check-in process on how well we are doing. In fact, rather than being a one-time, one-off, improvement project, it can be part of an ongoing, repeated check-in on whatever we are trying to improve now. Once we have fixed x, what can we tackle next? The permanent agenda item then becomes one of a continuous commitment to make the workplace better.

Do periodic success checks. In addition to regular feedback, what will be the markers of successful progress? As we mentioned earlier, it is important to be able to articulate *what will success look like,* in terms of the final match goal, so that everyone understands what the change is planning to achieve. But the path toward that goal is likely to have some noteworthy signposts along the way that indicate the achievement of successive targets. For example, if a staff lounge is being renovated, then there will be several steps in the process (such as removal of the old stuff, preparing the place for upgrades in painting the walls or installing equipment, moving in new furniture, and so on). Checking in on how well each of these stages is going, and whether some adjustments or modifications need to be made, will help keep things on track and still moving clearly toward the specific goal.

Internal and External Resources

So far, we have been talking about the process of creating better matches as something that can be done in-house, as an internal process of the work organization. There are many benefits to making workplace changes in this way, but there are also benefits to bringing in outside professional expertise to manage this kind of job improvement. Given that both have value, here are some issues to consider.

The primary rationale for an internal process of managing workplace changes is that people feel that they know themselves better than anyone else, so they can fix any internal problems better than anyone else. "We can do it with more value, and with less cost" is the underlying philosophy. Continuous improvement should come from within, from those who understand it best.

This approach is often coupled with the belief that outside services will not understand the specific occupation or organization and will only rely on stereotypes and the "same old" assumptions about people who work in that industry. Consequently, the concern is that outsiders will only be able to offer generic solutions that are not tailored to the actual workers. Moreover, these outside services will cost a lot more money but won't be able to deliver solid information. "Why hire some outsiders to tell us what we already know, and to charge us a lot of money for that?"

The contrasting view is that outside professional services can provide more comprehensive assessments and consultation on various kinds of organizational issues, largely because they have knowledge of strategies that have been used successfully elsewhere. This kind of service can be particularly helpful in situations where there are sensitive issues. It may be that people feel stuck and cannot work together well without help—especially if there has been chronic incivility among staff. Professional consultants are far more likely to have informed opinions about what measures to use and which programs to adopt, but of course there is a price to be paid for their perspective. It is important, too, when bringing in outside professionals to work on organizational changes, to ensure that their work is well integrated with the internal view of an initiative's goals and processes. If, for example, a decision has been made to start small, or a vision has been articulated of what success will look like, or a process has been established to have progress checkpoints happen at certain intervals, the consultants' work should align appropriately.

And now, after redesigning a better match, how do we translate that into reality? The critical aspects of implementing a change process are described in Chapter 11, illustrated by a work group process for improving the quality of employees' social relationships with each other. This approach is one way of responding to mismatches in *community*. It is noteworthy in focusing on improving the match between people and their jobs, as experienced through the social interactions among workers while carrying out their job tasks. It is a fully collaborative project, requiring active participation from management and members of the work groups.

11

Making Matches Work

If burnout arises from mismatches between people and their work situations, intervention means changing those relationships. As we have noted throughout this book, flexibility and a sense of agency regarding how, when, and where to work help people to maintain constructive and fulfilling relationships with their jobs. These qualities allow people to work out better matches both by changing the situation to better suit the way they want to work and by adapting how they work to better fit their job situation. In parallel, the same qualities allow workplaces to take effective action. With adequate flexibility and agency, managers can respond appropriately to employees encountering mismatches. Searching for solutions always entails a bit of back and forth. There must be ongoing dialogue.

Some current interventions have the good intention of reducing burnout but do not actually tackle the mismatch. Rather, their goal is to improve employees' capacity to *tolerate* mismatches. The hope is that the individual stress response can be successfully managed, even when the conditions aggravating the stress response remain unchanged. The implicit assumption is that the problem is in the "canary"—not in the demands of the workplace but in the limitations of people to manage those demands. To the extent that these approaches address relationships with work, they do so by focusing on one side of the relationship—the person—and leave the other side, the "coal mine" of the workplace, unchanged.

If a workplace is a benign setting with standards that most people readily accept as reasonable, then encouraging employees to tolerate and adapt to their situations at work makes sense. But if a workplace is fundamentally at odds with employees' needs and desires, as contemporary workplaces are often viewed as being, then advising people to tolerate or adapt to their situations amounts to encouraging surrender in a critical struggle. Since the rise of Industrial Revolution factories in the 1800s, people have tried to make their workplaces more compatible with human limitations and aspirations. Current conditions reflect significant gains brought about by concerted and extended action. Considerable gaps persist, however, as reflected in job insecurity, huge differences in executive compensation relative to employee pay, and unreasonable demands. Most mismatches do not come down to shortcomings in employees' approaches to work; they can be attributed to workplace structures and processes.

Conditions of Successful Change Processes

Improving the relationships people have with their workplaces is complicated. It calls for active participation from employees as well as adjustments by leaders across the six critical areas of the job-person relationship—workload, control, rewards, community, fairness, and values. Although it might be simpler for managers to implement an across-the-board workplace health program, or for an employee to engage in one stress-reduction technique like practicing mindfulness, real change comes through multiple, diverse improvements in how people interact with their work and how workplaces interact with their people. Simultaneous interventions in various areas of work life produce many effects in day-to-day interactions that add up to more engaging, positive matches and relationships with more potential for growth. Given both the complexity and the emotional charge of workplace change, it is important that such projects be implemented thoughtfully and thoroughly.

We've found that, in any area of work life, customizing interventions to recognize the unique circumstances of people and workplaces produces the most significant and lasting change. No work group is the same as another; every culture has been shaped by its own identities and backgrounds. Different people want different things from their work, and different workplaces have different expectations of their people. Our work on workplace change has identified six qualities of successful interventions: they are urgent, targeted, sustained, collaborative, evaluated, and timely. We'll spend a little time on each of these before outlining, in the second half of the chapter, a template approach to addressing community mismatches.

Without attention to these qualities, an initiative may work only haphazardly, or be ignored despite being implemented—or indeed, never get off the ground at all. Initiatives to improve the fit of people and workplaces must overcome the forces that originally brought about the mismatches. Work environments are not "naturally occurring"—they arise from deliberate decisions and investments, and the effects of past commitments can continue to exert influence after people have decided to change things. Even when no one deliberately intends to resist change, there is resistance in the form of inertia. Because clear sailing cannot be assumed, it is important in the planning and implementation of an initiative to build in these six qualities.

URGENT: WHY ACT NOW?

The first quality of a successful intervention is that it is made with a sense of urgency. Any established work setting has momentum that keeps it rolling along on the course it has already been taking. Only a perceived need for urgent change can generate enough energy to nudge it in a different direction. Urgency can arise from the pull of positive aspirations or from the push of negative pressures.

Aspirational urgency comes from an organization's commitment to its core values. When a leadership team is deeply committed to a value—whether it is environmental sustainability or respect among people or healthful living—its decisions give priority to that value over other choices that could be made or more expedient ways of doing business. Pressure urgency comes from the discomforts of a workplace's shortcomings. Employee complaints about mismatches, whether through official channels or personal conversations with supervisors, generate pressure to change. The urgent pressure to change can also come from external bodies, such as government regulators and outside sources of funding and accreditation, which often monitor performance in terms of employee health and other workplace issues.

Whether urgency is channeled through aspirations or pressures, it must be sufficient to overcome the many factors that favor continuation of the status quo. The first of these is that change *involves financial cost*, often in the form of consulting fees, and always in terms of staff time required to design and roll out a new program. Beyond this, change *demands managerial attention*—often a scarce resource in organizations as managers must simultaneously attend to other initiatives and responsibilities. For employees, too, any new program *competes with other programs* trying to engage their participation. It is common these days for employees to feel oversurveyed, for example, and workplaces typically offer many organized ways for people to improve their health, build their capabilities, and engage with colleagues. The context of past programs may also mean a new initiative *confronts a skepticism barrier*. People who have seen management fads come and go may have the cynical expectation that "this too shall pass," and invest little energy to make the change work.

In sum, all these factors can add up to the argument that it is easier to just continue what is already happening. To overcome that inertia, a sense of urgency is essential—yet this does not mean that the need for collaboration and customization can be bypassed. These may seem more time-consuming, and therefore at odds with the need for fast response implied by an urgent situation. But that need not be the case where the sense of urgency is based on a shared understanding of a group's greatest aspirations and worst pressure points. When an initiative starts out as a contentious process, contradictory views and aims can put it at risk; even if the project continues, it may struggle to maintain its focus. But having consensus at the outset about the pressures and aspirations motivating the project provides a foundation for collaborative, concerted, and sustained action. It leads to a response customized to address those particular hopes and concerns, and consolidates enough momentum to get things going in the right direction.

TARGETED: THE POINT OF THE ACTION

Any workplace initiative needs to get to the point and clearly convey the value it will deliver—and not only because people are busy. Beyond being distracted by other matters, they may actively doubt that leaders have their best interests in mind. They may have experienced workplace initiatives in the past that seriously missed their mark. To establish momentum, it matters that an initiative is strategically targeted.

Targeted initiatives are customized to the particular people and workplaces they will serve. To inspire action, initiatives need to target issues that matter to the people involved. Broad propositions to build healthier workplaces are generally less compelling than actions targeting distinct mismatches. Recall the story in Chapter 4 of a work group's agreeing on a certain block of time that would be free of meetings. It was not a solution that would apply to every work group, but it addressed a distinct need of that one, given its specific challenges in managing work demands.

SUSTAINED: THE FORM OF THE ACTION

Relationships with work improve slowly, and the gains made can prove fragile. Any initiative to fight burnout calls for an ongoing commitment to see it through and to follow up the initial implementation with supportive action as needed. Often, what looks like a quick fix turns out to be more complicated. For example, replacing an autocratic leader with one who solicits others' input does not lead immediately to more inclusive decision-making by a work unit. Changing the executive is a step, but people need to settle into a sense of psychological safety and develop the capacity to frame and solve problems to collectively arrive at good decisions. Initiatives need persistent attention to spot unexpected complications that may emerge and to address the deeper dynamics involved.

COLLABORATIVE: SHARED ACTION

We noted above that it matters how leaders introduce organizational initiatives. A thorough process is shared and cooperative, and includes conversations with potential participants to determine their goals. The process needs to come across as responsive to the mismatches that people feel in their work lives. To the extent that it fails to resonate with an employee's experience of a job-person mismatch, it will not engage that person in the change effort.

Collaboration cannot start too early, but it can certainly start too late. An essential initial step is to listen as people describe the problems they are facing and use what they say to shape how the process will unfold. The next step, again working together, is to generate possible goals and strategies to attain those objectives—and collaboration continues to matter through implementation and evaluation. The stories in Chapter 6 about improving recognition—the computer-based workplace that resolved the mismatch on rewards with a new financing plan for employees, and the department that decided to spend money on a staff lounge instead of the staff picnic lunch—drew their strength entirely from collaboration. The more top-down structures of the previous systems were well intended. They did not, however, establish the necessary resonance with the active involvement of the affected employees in the design and implementation of the new system.

EVALUATED: EVIDENCE OF ACTION

Establishing an evidence-based approach to management requires systematic monitoring of conditions and experiences. This means evaluating work groups before and after an intervention, and at a later follow-up, to assess the persistence of its outcomes. When possible, effects are measured against the experience of comparison groups that have not implemented the process.

One form of accounting for a project's impact is the use of pre- and post-intervention surveys. The initial survey defines the starting point for the group, and the second survey captures any gains (or losses). Do people have a more positive experience of their workplace after going through the process?

Beyond the findings of such surveys, the very willingness of people to complete them provides some indication of a work group's readiness for change. A low participation rate weakens a survey's validity, but it also suggests that people lack the will or ability to collaborate on a change initiative. Their reticence may be rooted in a lack of trust or simply reflect an unsuccessful communication strategy. Or it could mean they do not value the intended goal enough to put in the effort. In contrast, strong levels of survey participation and active engagement with information about the project indicate sufficient urgency among work group members to anticipate the commitment needed to see the project through.

TIMELY: RESPONSIVE ACTION

Readiness for change can be fleeting. We have seen this, for example, in survey efforts. Designed to capture ideas, feelings, and perceptions that cannot be deduced by watching people, surveys often prompt people to reflect more deeply on a problem. The process of drawing their attention to a mismatch and generating responses can make them more eager to see it addressed. There is value in minimizing the elapsed time between fielding a survey and reporting on its results—and then visibly acting on the findings. Quick turnaround is especially vital because survey projects often fail to generate action that feels meaningful to participants. It does not take long for already skeptical people to conclude that nothing will come of an effort.

Timely need not mean *rushed*, however. It can take a while for members of a work group to concur that they have a problem. For example, after a workplace bully has departed from the work group, it may take people a while to realize that that individual's behavior reflected a deeper problem with the workplace culture that would continue to aggravate community mismatches. Finding the best time for action requires sensitivity to the work group's experience. Finding the right moment to act requires close attention to people and their situations.

The huddles in the healthcare setting described in Chapter 7— the "cuddle-huddles" at the beginning of a group's shift—were an effective response to a pressing need for emotional support. Their timeliness derived partly from the fact that the initiative was entirely within the work group's domain. They did not need approval from management to introduce this practice. The need for support translated directly into a means of providing that support.

With these parameters in mind, much progress can be made on addressing mismatches. A collaborative process means that the people and the workplaces implementing the process are the ones who are to benefit from the process. A sincere intention to improve behavior or a situation does not, however, always translate into effective action. Some mismatches call for additional expertise or another perspective to move things in the right direction.

AN APPROACH TO ADDRESSING COMMUNITY MISMATCHES

Although a work group can at times act effectively on its own to address problems with its group culture, some situations can remain intractable. There are work groups with long-term conflicts that undermine the trust necessary to collaborate. Some social encounters have such powerful emotional dynamics that people find them too risky to address. In our previous work we found that employees who volunteered to facilitate work group civility processes lacked the authority and experience necessary to help participants resolve especially fraught encounters that arose in the sessions. An external facilitator can bring needed expertise and a capacity to promote the psychological safety required to work together.

One example of a facilitated process for improving the social dynamics of a work group is called Strengthening a Culture of Respect and Engagement (SCORE).[1] In this kind of intervention, intact work groups—people who share a manager and who interact regularly with one another—reflect on their social dynamics as a step toward changing how they encounter one another. In many ways, this is the equivalent of family therapy for work groups.

The process begins with a baseline survey of a work group's social dynamics, then proceeds through a series of group sessions. These sessions occur several weeks apart, because groups need time between these meetings to try out new ways of interacting with one another, as part of the "homework assignments." After the completion of all the sessions, there is a matched post-intervention survey that assesses the subsequent changes in the group's social dynamics.

A facilitator plays a pivotal role in leading a deep dive into these group processes. In addition to standard roles of sharing information and encouraging group participation, the facilitators work with encounters among people within the session. Since some relationships among people in sessions can be emotionally charged and have been for a long time, unpacking the dynamics of these exchanges requires a firm but delicate approach. Another point of collaboration are co-facilitators, who are employees of the organization who are familiar with the work group but not usually members of it. They know the workplace culture and they work on-site to maintain continuity during the weeks between sessions. Their active participation becomes a means of knowledge transfer.

To illustrate how a better match is made in the area of community, let's take a more detailed look at a recent use of the process. Work groups from a variety of workplaces in Australia—in health care, policing, firefighting, broadcasting, financial services, and government—implemented this kind of work group process. This section focuses primarily on a hospital in an urban setting that implemented the process in multiple work groups.

Several years ago in Australia, a major government report, "Bullying and Harassment in the Health Sector," looked into mistreatment of employees within public health services and found serious lapses in how leaders of health sector agencies responded to reports of unreasonable behavior: "The leadership—the board and executive of audited agencies—currently has inadequate governance and oversight of the risk posed by bullying and harassment. Although the leadership has a duty of care to its employees under OHS [Occupational Health and Safety] legislation, bullying and harassment is not given the level of priority the seriousness of the risk demands."[2]

Words like these got the attention of healthcare agency leaders. In addition to calling them out explicitly for failing to realize even the minimum standards of their ideals, the reference to neglecting "duty of care" implied a liability risk. A government audit is, of course, a very consequential pressure source for any public sector workplace, and there was a clear sense of urgency to find solutions. In one hospital, the report was especially timely because the hospital had already been reviewing its procedures for responding to employee complaints of mistreatment at work. The report on bullying and harassment made it all the more important to respond to the problem in a timely manner. This hospital, as part of a broader initiative to improve work group cultures, decided to contract with an outside consultant to help work groups reporting such breakdowns in their work communities.

The focus on finding solutions for specific work groups rather than the entire organization allowed for the most timely response. The objective was to make immediate improvements in the quality of colleagues' day-to-day social interactions, which would create a climate to support increasingly positive ongoing dynamics among work group members. This was accomplished through a series of five group sessions, convened at three-week intervals, with the expectation that the few weeks following each session would be used by the group to consciously engage in the activities and behaviors modeled in the sessions. Used in other settings since, these SCORE sessions represent an effective way to, within a few months, begin to inculcate more respectful behavior, after which follow-up sessions, if desired, can reinforce the learning. The sessions are briefly described here.

Acknowledging respect (Session 1). The first session uses the results from the initial survey as a launching point for discussing the current state of the work group. The conversation explores why respect matters and guides the group's identification of goals for improvement. The method's open-ended questions permit work groups to propose and have the final say on specific goals to target, based on their particular concerns. In this first gathering, the group also agrees on ground rules for their work in this process.

In the hospital, the participating groups were ones with members reporting what we call serious mismatches in the "community" dimension of their work, typically involving strained power relationships. Patterns of interaction among some members suggested that others did not have equal membership in the group. In effect, group "insiders" treated other members as outsiders. In the initial session where this was brought to light, the result was a consensus decision to set two goals: to establish balance among the people in the work group, and to establish norms by which respect and consideration would be the dominant pattern against which rudeness would occur rarely and with little power.

The participating work groups set specific targets of behaviors they intended to change during the process. For example, one group was concerned with increasing the extent to which they used active listening skills. They acknowledged that some interactions needed to be short and to the point during their workdays, but felt that too many of their encounters were forced into that mode. They also wanted to reduce negative gossip about one another. In the session, the work group committed to developing a culture that more strongly conveyed a unity of purpose, aligning more strongly with the core values of the hospital. The openness of the process allowed for a timely response to the work groups' current concerns.

Unity of purpose was important early in the process. One way that greater unity was established was through the method of creating ground rules for the sessions. The process asked everyone individually to state whether they agreed with the slate of ground rules the group had just compiled for itself. With everyone on record, these ground rules then served as a unified, shared reference point to which facilitators could appeal in moments of friction or resistance. The process of establishing ground rules in itself set a model for how the rest of the sessions would operate. As a facilitator put it, "I needed to ensure that others felt safe to discuss what they needed to discuss and were not threatened or cajoled by others when the discussion went into difficult territory. The ground rules were a helpful mechanism to increase psychological safety." In the long run, practicing respect in day-to-day encounters conveyed a sense of unity much more deeply than making proclamations to that effect.

Promoting respect (Session 2). As the second session convenes, participants have just spent three weeks doing the "homework" of tracking their instances of initiating positive interactions at work. This session is about building on those gains and committing to increasing their rate of civility. Small, incremental increases are encouraged. The agenda for Session 2 includes role-plays in which people first act out a scenario in which a request is made in an inconsiderate manner and then a scenario where the same request is made civilly. A defining quality of SCORE is that it is active; people *do* the process—it is not done to them. In this way, collaboration is the essence of the process. It means that participants have to do the work. Sitting back and watching the facilitator go through her (or his) paces is not an option. To note, participation is not actually everyone's favored way of doing things. The fact that a collaborative process has the best results in the long run does not immediately translate into people enthusiastically embracing participation. Some effort must go into charming participants into talking and even getting out of their seats and moving around. In interviews after completing the process, participants and facilitators reflected on what they perceived as the active ingredients of the process. Generally, they identified the active participation of people in the session as the driving force.

A primary focus of Session 2 was on the power of reciprocity in generating change. People easily recognized that rude behavior generated more of the same. They needed to stay with the issue longer to accept that they could generate more respect by actively respecting and appreciating others. Participation in the role-plays was an important part of that realization. They learned that each person's civility could nudge things in the right direction; as a team working together, they could have a significant impact. "When the groups were sharing stories about respect," one participant noted, "there seemed to be a lot of positivity in the room and acknowledgment of others' respectful behavior; for example, 'I really appreciate it when J. helps me out when she sees that I am really busy.'"

"But you know," this participant continued, "those role-plays were a really important thing. I think they're important to have those. Do that little bit of homework part, but then do the role-play so people can experience it and know what it's like to be able to share. So, if you've got somebody who's very reserved and quiet and has issues in expressing maybe their feelings because of whatever, it's good to get them into that sort of scenario."

Responding to disrespect (Session 3). The group members consider constructive ways of responding to instances of disrespect, either through direct interaction or situations they have observed. They commit to doing so in the following weeks. This approach is especially suited to healthcare settings that build much of their practice around evidence-based medical protocols. They develop confidence that following a set of procedures gives the best results. An agreed-upon protocol also makes an encounter less personal. When calling out wrong behaviors, people can also assure a colleague, "I'm not trying to give you a hard time." They are only doing what was agreed on in the session.

Importantly, even when clearly engaging in role-play, people had mental and physical responses to receiving incivility. The situations took on the sense of reality in the moment. People felt genuinely angry when someone pretended to treat them badly. Also in the role-plays people received feedback on expressions of civility and incivility about which they were previously unaware. A co-facilitator shared her view of success factors: "the role-play . . . I think that was probably the most important part. People were really slow to get into that, and my colleague and I would move around the groups and do it. 'I'll go first,' you know—try and lighten it up and get them to do it. I think that helped because they were a little bit, 'Oh, god' . . . . I think it was really good that [one of the role-plays] was not in a health setting. The fact that it was an office setting—so, you can equate, but it's not exactly the same. You're not involving a patient or patient's family."

Each of these statements note active participation in the process by members of the work groups. They reflect dialogue among people in the session. Participants do not passively absorb information from the facilitator but contribute their experiences and insights.

People realize through the process that they cannot leave it to others to look after their social relationships, nor can they have unilateral control over the social relationships of others. In this way, the process defines a shared way of working together afterward.

Working regardless of disrespect (Session 4). Although members of the work group commit to improving civility, promoting courtesy may continue to be an uphill slog for a long time. The fourth session explores ways of persevering and supporting one another as the work group continues to promote positive behavior.

Hospital settings have challenges in their interactions with other parts of their complex organizations. For example, people in laboratory services receive calls from emergency and intensive care that presume that shouting is a strategy for getting quicker service. The laboratory personnel have limited capacity to determine how people behave in those other units, but they can respond to rude behavior in ways that discourage it.

The manager of one of the units related that she had caught herself being dismissive of a student nurse who asked a question relating to her placement. The unit manager reflected, after the student had left sheepishly, that she was not fulfilling her role as a mentor or as a professional modelling civil behavior at work. She promptly followed the student to where she was working to apologize. "I told her to come to me whenever she had questions. It was my job to be there for her, and I take that responsibility seriously."

One of the participants complimented one of his colleagues for responding effectively to a rude person encountered the previous day. He noted that his colleague had remained calm, maintained eye contact, and made firm use of their agreed-upon phrase: "I can't hear you when you shout at me. We need to take it down a notch."

These sorts of self-disclosures were not easy for people to make in a meeting with their coworkers. In these sessions, the facilitators supported psychological safety by encouraging people to take risks and supporting them when they did so. Each of these statements prompted a process of reflection on how the incident fit with the group's hopes for its development as a work group culture. Having a positive attitude did not always suffice; support often required active involvement.

Integrating respect into work life (Session 5). In the final session, the group considers ways of integrating what they have learned into the ongoing life of the work group. They may develop policies or rituals that maintain the momentum they have gained.

In the hospital work groups, the process went beyond providing information to setting up situations that brought about self-reflection. Although insight alone is not enough to change a workplace culture, without insight progress becomes fragile. Insight provided participants with the capacity to respond appropriately when they encountered difficult situations during their work.

An integral part of the hospital process occurred in the final session in which participants developed ways of sustaining their gains from the process. One action was adding an ongoing agenda item on civility and respect to all of the work units' formal meetings. A group decided to maintain interactive posters on which people indicated the social weather report for the day, including sunny cheerfulness or stormy discord. These activities provided a psychologically safe channel for commenting on the work unit's dynamics. Another work group suggested policy changes on handling formal complaints at the hospital.

The process did not strive to erase all acts of rudeness or inconsideration from work life. After all, one person's constructive criticism is another person's uncalled-for insult. These encounters, however, provided occasions to work out paths to better understanding. One group strived to establish a more peaceful rhythm in their conversations: rather than focusing on what to say next, they hoped to slow down to listen more thoroughly to what the other person was saying. The program did strive to establish a rhythm in which incivility occurs against a background of respect. For well-functioning work groups, that ratio is 90 percent respect, but it is rarely a perfect 100 percent.

Measuring change: Post-session assessment. The central finding of an assessment is the extent to which the process successfully achieved its desired change. Since this may not be intuitively obvious, and although it is important to talk with individuals and small groups about their perceptions, those conversations may not tell the full story. For this reason, we turn to surveys.

Accurate surveys have been validated as giving a reliable assessment. Even when the real interest is a downstream impact, such as improving fairness to reduce burnout, it is important to evaluate what exactly the process intends to change. For example, if the process is meant to increase transparency of promotion processes, it is important to determine whether people are confident that they receive better information about how such decisions are made. The process is more solid when it not only reduces cynicism, but when that reduction reflects greater transparency in decision-making.

The process was evaluated from multiple perspectives to validate it as an evidence-based management initiative. Surveys occurred before and after the process. They also replicated the survey with other work groups at the hospital, for comparison. Further, there were interviews with participants and facilitators to capture their perceptions of the process and to identify elements that had an impact on people when they were participating. The initial survey in the first session helped to specify the areas of concern, and the survey afterward provided a gauge of impact for the participants and for those in workplace leadership who supported the program.

In the responses from the first and second surveys, the hospital work groups saw evidence that progress had been made toward their goal of improving the workplace culture. The initial survey for one of the participating work groups showed lower-than-average frequencies in three areas: positive encounters, acknowledging others, and expressing appreciation. The group had also reported a higher-than-average frequency of disrespectful encounters. After the process, more frequent expressions of respect showed up on the Social Encounters Scale.[3]

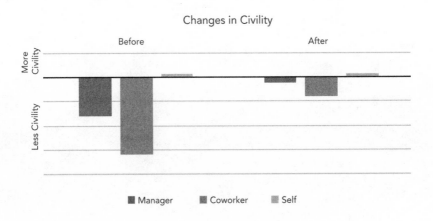

These colleagues also reported less frequent disrespect in their social encounters.

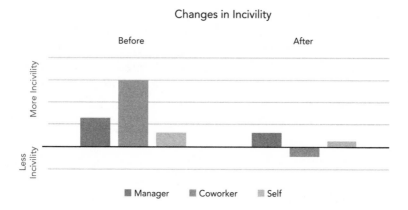

Changes in Incivility

Other work groups that had not participated in SCORE remained unchanged in their expressions of respect and disrespect.

Other surveys used the Maslach Burnout Inventory.[4] These also revealed that burnout had decreased, while indicators of engagement increased.

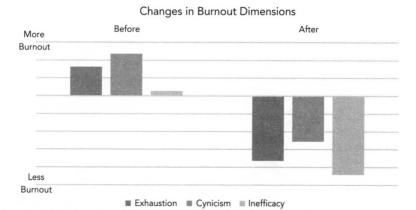

Changes in Burnout Dimensions

Exhaustion and cynicism had declined, with participants reporting more energy and involvement with their work and with the people around them. They also indicated that they felt more effective in their work.

The outcome was a work group culture that increased people's matches with their workplace. The healthcare group had noted ways in which power was unbalanced within their work group: it varied with people's age, tenure, credentials, friendships, access to information, gender, clique membership, and where they usually sat during meetings. The group intended to develop a culture that appreciated everyone's contribution. A key objective of the SCORE program was to restore balance in their social exchanges at work. This striving for balance functioned as an immediate goal during the sessions, as an intermediate goal in the "putting into practice" exercises that occurred between sessions, and as a long-term goal in the group's aspirations for the future, after it had completed the program.

As we've seen, not only in this example but throughout the previous chapters, people can work together to tweak parts of their work routine to remove annoyances and inefficiencies. Supervisors can coach employees to improve their effectiveness or develop flexible schedules that help employees accommodate the demands they encounter. Work groups can embark on processes that improve their team cultures, allowing them to make stronger contributions to their workplaces with less discord and distraction. Entire workplaces can embark on a process of revamping their policies and structures to establish flexibility and a sense of agency throughout. The possibilities for better matches between workers and their workplace are vast. No single solution will encompass all those possibilities, so multiple and continuing approaches are always needed.

Bringing about fulfilling matches at work requires an openness to people *collaborating* with workplace leadership, flexibility to *customize* policies and procedures to fit work group cultures, and *commitment* to core values of respect, workplace well-being, and fulfilling jobs. As work becomes increasingly uncoupled from time and place, it remains an intrinsically social activity. The capacity to work together, to provide leadership, and to communicate with clarity and respect becomes increasingly important.

12

Meeting the Challenge of Burnout

The time has come to rethink how and why people work, and how to make workplaces environments in which all workers can thrive. This requires more than simply changing the workers' capacity to work anywhere at any hour of any day. Since work takes up a lot of people's time, talent, and potential, the workplace should offer more in return, in terms of a sustainable and rewarding quality of life.

We do not claim to have a single best practice or a guaranteed solution for getting rid of burnout. Rather, we have shared many important lessons about what burnout is, why it occurs, and what positive changes can be made. If you take these lessons to heart and start putting them into practice, you can make progress toward making the experience of work more fulfilling, motivating, and viable—for yourself or, as a manager, for others in your organization.

We have spent decades researching workplace challenges and know that burnout is the name people give to their experience of trying to function well in challenging situations but having difficulty in doing so. It is an experience that has adverse and costly consequences, not only for the individuals feeling burned out, but for those they encounter both at work and home. And, contrary to how other people use the word, burnout is not solely an individual's issue. It is a relationship issue between an individual and the workplace.

The concept of a job-person match focuses on the *relationship* between the individual person and the situational job context. It is a mistake to focus on just one side or the other as the sole source of blame for burnout or the sole source of solutions for this problem. The biased tendency to focus just on the person, rather than the situation, has led to the misguided assumption that burnout is just an individual weakness or illness or flaw, and that individual-based solutions are the only answer. By taking a broader and more accurate view of the individual *in context*, however, the strong intersection of both personal and situational factors becomes far more evident. Consequently, the strategy of enhancing the job-person fit between workers and their workplaces becomes far more compelling, as we illustrated through actual stories about workplaces that have found ways to act on these issues.

As you've seen, burnout tells us more about the challenging situations than it does about the individual who is trying to deal with them. It has pointed to some core characteristics of all situations, which are critical in terms of people's behaviors, motives, and growth. Importantly, it has underscored that the *match*, or *fit*, between the person and these core job aspects is the key to understanding burnout—as well as the other work profiles we discussed, including disengaged, overextended, ineffective, and engaged.

The core domains of job-person match—capability, social, and moral—affect people's skill in completing the job tasks effectively, working with others successfully, and doing the right things throughout. In the capability domain, the key areas involve *workload* and *control*; in the social domain, *community* and *rewards* are the significant areas; and in the moral domain, *fairness* and *values* carry most weight. Achieving better fits in all these areas is the path to achieving a more engaged workforce.

Positive changes to achieve better matches can be done in many ways—there is no single, limited, one-size-fits-all solution. They can involve any number of the six areas of work life, they can involve small changes as well as large ones, they can vary in financial cost from none to a lot, and they can be done within smaller groups or teams or units, as well as within an entire organization. They take time and effort, but they are worth it. And they will all benefit from following the three C's: collaboration (asking all employees to be a part of making things better), customization (adapting a proposed change to the local culture and type of occupation), and commitment (sustaining the effort to achieve positive improvements).

Lessons Learned for Making Better Matches

First, we need to look for the crucial gaps and mismatches. We know to look at both sides of those mismatches, both the person and the job, to find ways to adjust and synchronize. As with any relationship problem, it takes two to tango. Everyone needs to consider both one's own and another's perspective, and work toward shared action.

What we also need to learn is that one positive adjustment will be good but never enough, so we need to set up a system of continuous improvement. The world is constantly changing, in many ways that are not always foreseeable, so there needs to be continuous adjustments to the new mismatches that will inevitably arise. There is no definitive solution to any particular problem, because the "problem" will keep morphing into something different, and thus require a different adjustment to close the gap. Just consider, for example, how the development of new technologies has changed the nature of the workplace, whether it involves assembly lines, or treatment of patients or customers, or international contract negotiations. Or consider how the Covid-19 pandemic changed many workplace offices to home ones and changed in-person meetings into virtual Zoom ones. The continuous challenge will always be how to improve the job-person match to maximize the advantages while adjusting to minimize the downsides, while in the midst of organizational or global change.

INDIVIDUAL CHANGE

Much of the individual approach to burnout has focused on *self-care,* like how to fix oneself to be stronger, healthier, and more resilient. Although those kinds of healthy coping strategies are important, they can be more successful if they are coordinated to fit with situational job constraints. For example, how can a person get more sleep or exercise or pursue a hobby, by working around the workload demands for overtime? By taking a deeper look at both job and person perspectives, however, an individual can focus more on *shared care* and identify alternative options for managing workload so that personal time is more protected from unexpected interruptions. Here are some other practical examples of using both person and job perspectives.

Seeing oneself in the job. To make the most of flexibility in one's relationship with work, it's important to know what truly matters. It helps to ask oneself some key questions about one's own match or mismatch with the job, and in what particular aspects. Where does one want to invest time and energy? When reflecting on the past week at work, what were the high points when one felt closest to doing what really matters? Did any of the domains—capability, social, or moral—play a large role in those moments? On the other end of the scale, did the low points over the past week relate to any of those domains?

Being flexible. Relationships thrive with flexibility on both sides. It is reasonable to expect workplaces to make an effort to accommodate the aspirations and constraints of people, but it is also important for people to accommodate the aspirations and constraints of workplaces. Situations are rarely perfect from the start. Relationships improve through experience and dialogue. A constructive response to a problem is to search for a resolution.

Modeling civility. Uncivil environments draw the worst from people. In the spur of the moment, responding rudely to someone who has just been rude to you may have its own emotional logic. Reciprocity has a compelling quality about it. But people can decide to pass on the urge to reciprocate with more rudeness. Sometimes nothing is the best thing to say. Sometimes the occasion allows for something more constructive.

Being appreciative. A bit of appreciation can go a long way. Some situations may call for ovations—for example, an opera singer has a bad night unless thunderous applause follows her aria. But in many situations a smile and a nod will suffice. Appreciation only feels overdone when it lacks sincerity.

Being persistent. Improving relationships with work not only takes a long time, but the nature of a great relationship with work constantly changes. This is the opposite of a short-term project. It's more like a lifestyle.

Being just cautious enough. There are certainly workplaces with rigid policies and little tolerance for individual preferences or aspirations. People have legitimate qualms about admitting to any difficulties in doing their work. For many, managers are sources of problems more often than sources of solutions. It helps, however, to have a clear-eyed understanding of the risks and opportunities. Although too much openness can get people into trouble, too much caution can keep them stuck longer than necessary. Be cautious but open to possibilities.

WORKPLACE CHANGE

When an organizational project identifies issues that are creating mismatches for employees, such as unfairness, value conflicts, or micromanagement, the results are seldom surprising. We rarely hear anyone respond, "Who could ever imagine micromanagement would contribute to burnout?" We rarely hear, "How could anyone feel unfairly treated here?" The responses are more along the lines of, "Of course. That makes sense." In short, job surveys do not often identify problems no one ever expected to find. They frequently confirm and, to some extent, quantify problems that many people were already aware of, even if, as in some cases, employees have not spoken out publicly about these concerns.

For these reasons, job assessment surveys are a good place to start. Often, the primary rationale for doing a survey project is to provide a foundation for taking action and to find out where action is needed most urgently. Rarely are job-person mismatches evenly distributed across a large organization. Most places manage some operations or processes much better than they manage others. In addition, if done well, a survey gives a strong (but anonymous) voice to everyone in the workplace, who can then raise concerns about a serious issue that no one is willing to talk about publicly. Furthermore, the survey can make all employees feel like collaborative partners in identifying what needs improvement and how to do it, which will make them more committed to seeing the project through.

Then, use the results from the survey to implement some changes. As we noted earlier, if employees provide answers to survey questions, but then never hear about the results and never see any constructive improvements emerge from them, they become even more cynical about the entire process. They may even refuse to be part of it in the future. Therefore, the assessments need to occur when there is a plan to act on the results. The important question is not "What is related to burnout?" That is already well known. Rather, the question should be "Of all the things related to burnout, what could we change?"

Most likely the biggest challenge will be determining how to foster ongoing, continuous improvements in job-person matches. How can we normalize a process of identifying actions for improvement and then implementing them? One answer is to convert it into a known model of regular assessment—the medical checkup. Most people are concerned about their own physical health over their lifespan, and they want to know how they can stay well and be able to do whatever they want in life. Consequently, they probably have a regular medical exam or checkup. This gives them an updated status report on what is healthy and working well, what is problematic and functioning poorly, and whether there are any warning signs of possible future problems that could be prevented. This is a normal, routine process that occurs on a regular timetable, every one or two years, to see how things are going and to make continued improvements and any helpful course corrections.

In a similar way, organizational change processes like the ones presented in earlier chapters can function like a regular checkup on organizational health by assessing the current state of an organization regarding the well-being of its workforce. It provides a method for assessing where people are engaged and working well, where people are burned out and functioning poorly, and what organizational issues need some attention. The goal of this kind of checkup is both constructive and future-oriented. "What can we do to get to a place that is better than where we are now?" In that sense, an organizational checkup is different from a report card type of appraisal, which is more evaluative and past-oriented: "How well have we done?"

Just like a medical checkup, an organizational checkup provides a more informed sense of what the problem areas are and where they are located. It does not yield specific solutions, per se. For example, a medical checkup might show that a person's cholesterol level is too high, but it does not specify what would be the best recommended solutions for this particular patient. Similarly, an organizational checkup might show a link between staff burnout and issues of fairness, such as pay equity. Although it can identify a problem that needs attention within the organization, it does not dictate what the organizational response should be. There are often many options for interventions that could improve things, so the good news is that there will always be a range of choices. Any intervention, however, must be tailored to the unique circumstances of a particular organization—there is no generic, one-size-fits-all solution for burnout and any of the six area mismatches.

If we follow the medical analogy, a checkup takes place annually. While it is not required for a workplace to do this annually, it should be done more than once. This allows the organization to track its growth and changes in terms of the well-being of its workforce: to assess how well things are going, whether interventions have yielded improvements, if there are new problems on the horizon, and so forth. It can also help prepare organizations for future change, such as a merger or downsizing, then aid them in managing that transition, and then follow up on its impact, both short- and long-term.

Just like a medical checkup, an organizational checkup should not take place only in a time of crisis. A checkup that is purely crisis-driven will not be viewed as a fair and impartial assessment of how things are going. Rather, it will be seen as a process to find problems and to find people to blame for them—and that will engender distrust and resistance, as well as fuel staff paranoia. Although a crisis may motivate an organization to address some of its immediate problems, a routine, repeated assessment is designed to be more far-reaching. The regularity of an organizational checkup can provide a long-term view of the organization and its responses to whatever challenges it faces. Ideally, then, organizational checkups should be part of an organization's commitment to the well-being of its workforce. If they are done periodically, on a routine basis, that commitment becomes an ongoing one—not only for the workforce as a whole, but for the leadership and the team who make the checkups happen.

FUTURE CHANGE

In 2020, the Covid-19 pandemic inflicted major change in how people worked. In critical sectors, the shifts were abrupt as workplaces strove to serve their patients, customers, students, clientele, or patrons while protecting the lives of their employees. The impact included sudden unemployment, high risk exposure to the public, and shifts from office to home. For some, demand plunged to nothing; for others, demand went to extreme intensity. Some settings failed miserably, others found their way through trial and error, while others landed on their feet. The shift was hard on many, and fatal to some. For the most part people rose to the occasion, adapted, and continued contributing under these disrupted conditions.

As 2021 progressed, there was something of an end in sight, but also realizations that how people work had changed forever. As workplaces reestablish in the years to come, we have an opportunity to develop something new and improved, an environment that positions workplaces and people to thrive. Success in managing that transition can have long-term implications for workplaces' capacity to attract and retain the needed talent. The situation we have found ourselves in calls for a broad perspective that accommodates psychological aspirations as well as productivity.

We must first recognize the value of this experience. The essence of resilience is to thrive while undergoing disruptions and distress. People learned a lot about themselves and the people around them during this process. They learned new ways of getting their work done. Some of what they've learned, such as the kinds of work they can complete better away from the office, provides opportunities for constructive change. To have an impact, people need to share this experience at work, and the workplace needs to respond in ways that derive value from these experiences.

We saw some "wins": ways that workplaces learned from pandemic disruption. In healthcare settings, clinicians learned better ways of responding to the virus, improving patients' recovery as they tested new approaches and shared the results. They also learned how to work together in newly formed teams as hospitals reconfigured work groups to shift capacity to where it was most needed. With a shift to extreme cases, hospitals realized that lessons learned could be applied to outpatient settings, and vice versa. The central point is that there is much to be gained in sharing what people have learned when adapting to the extreme circumstances of the pandemic. Major crises provide an opportunity to reflect on how to do things better than what used to be the status quo. They also provide opportunities to reflect on why some changes do *not* work better; it is important to keep in mind that we can learn a lot from mistakes and failures, especially if they resulted from efforts with the best of intentions.

The segment of the population that was able to work from home brought up several potential mismatches and issues, as well as opportunities for future community problem solving. For those working remotely during the pandemic, the experience and its implications for burnout have been mixed. For one, the opportunity for remote work was available to only a segment of the workforce, while others either lost their jobs or continued to work in place, often with exposure to infection. For another, some people worked at homes that were spacious, private, and well equipped with furniture and Wi-Fi. Other people worked at homes that were cramped, crowded, and poorly equipped. Some people worked alone, some with other adults in the same living space, and others had children who required childcare or homeschooling. Having portable work does not say anything about the location to which the work is taken. Despite challenges, an aggregation of national polls found that most people report that remote work maintains or even increases their productivity.[1] Other polls around the same time found employers to be more skeptical, however, with less agreement about a boost to productivity, but still only a minority reporting perceived decreases in productivity.

Many employers leaned toward a future with a mixture of remote and on-site work. A widely expressed view was that physical presence both builds a stronger workplace culture and positions individuals better for promotion and other opportunities. In short, those out of sight would soon be out of mind. This view fits with the model of senior managers as having highly fragmented days, moving from one issue to the next, making quick decisions along the way. Whoever is standing nearby will be burdened with associated demands, some of which turn into great opportunities. Such managers are unlikely to take the effort to recall and contact a staff member working remotely.

Clearly, the post-pandemic transition presents possibilities and perils. On the positive side, some families experienced the positive effects of having parents spending more time at home (albeit often on Zoom), rather than traveling to offices or flying to distant cities. Some employees found that they were working more effectively from home than they had been at the office. For example, one lawyer talked about how his client interviews were much better when they were done online: "Do you think it's *because* I'm in my sweats?" The boundary of work and nonwork became even fuzzier, however, when working at home. The commute, despite its well-deserved reputation for drudgery, provided a temporal and spatial buffer that strengthened the distinction between work identity and personal identity. Eliminating the commute brought benefits, but it also resulted in weakening that separation.[2] It also raised the question of how much of previous commuting time became work time and how much became personal time. Recovered commuting time could have been the source of increased productivity. But employers have always treated commuting as personal time, not time for which people were being paid. In the other direction, working at home presented more opportunities for personal issues to impinge on work time.

Such issues of time and place are relationship issues. Anticipating their benefits and burdens will avoid many problematic hassles for people as a transition unfolds. Leaders and employees should collaborate to develop a shared understanding. A situation like this calls for creative thinking that customizes solutions to the distinct qualities of the job and to the personal lives of those involved. It calls for commitment to a new equilibrium with reasonable demands that are fully recognized.

Workplaces with a mix of remote and on-site modes need to anticipate fairness issues that could arise from new configurations. One issue is the question of who must work on-site and how often. For people with inconvenient, long, expensive commutes, the option to work from home would have value. Clearly, some workers need to be on-site at a workplace: tending a checkout or cutting hair requires physical presence. Other jobs are less straightforward, and a mix of on-site and remote work could work well at least some of the time. As with the example of the distinguished service award in Chapter 8, people have a deeper sense of fairness with an open decision-making process. A collaborative process involving managers and members of work groups would establish the parameters for working remotely that would make sense to the people affected by the policy. This conversation may also anticipate ways of offsetting the downside of remote working: a lack of presence in the workplace. A work group would develop processes for acknowledging contributions to the work group's efforts that can encompass everyone regardless of location. This kind of process supports ongoing commitment because it is more susceptible to being monitored to ensure that outcomes are consistent with the policy.

The location itself can be mismatched with the requirements to manage workload. A consequence of a location-centric view of work is that employers view the furnishing, equipping, and connecting of remote home sites as the employees' private responsibility. Sitting for a long time in an ergonomic office chair can be tolerable, but sitting on a simple kitchen stool for hours at a time, day after day, is damaging to the human body. Although people managed jury-rigged solutions in the first throes of the pandemic, this is not a model for going forward. The potential for mismatches is huge during transitions in work life. They call for ongoing dialogue as people learn about the possibilities and limitations of their innovations and unanticipated mismatches emerge.

The need for strong workplace cultures also reflects relationship issues in the community area. Work group cultures encompass assumptions, expectations, and behaviors about online communications. Are there consequences, explicit or implicit, for not attending a Zoom meeting? Is it important for each participant to say something during each meeting? Is it important to mute audio when not speaking? Is it okay to turn off video? On messaging, is it important to acknowledge receiving each message, or can it go without saying? In short, members of work groups may have assumptions and expectations of one another's behavior. Without work groups taking time to talk through the ground rules for remote communications, individuals can offend one another or miss important cues without being aware there was ever an issue. In addition to virtual meetings, remote work creates more occasions for one-on-one communications. Some of these communications can be instances of intimidating or offensive encounters because they are unmonitored.[3] As with the SCORE approach, workplaces can use a collaborative process to anticipate potential community mismatches to create solutions customized to their work group cultures. With a firm commitment to respectful workplace policies, virtual communications can create psychologically safe environments that support a diverse workforce in a variety of locations.

The varied experience of people during the pandemic and its aftermath increases the potential for value mismatches. The first step in collaborating on values is acknowledging that everyone is not starting on the same page. Some people have endured profound loss; others have been at most inconvenienced. Further, some people have had to make hard choices, while others have had to enforce hard choices made by others. For example, healthcare professionals reported distress when enforcing their facilities' policies forbidding family visits to critically ill relatives. Regardless of the professionals' moral judgment about the policies' benefits in preventing contagion, enforcing the policies often created stress. Acknowledging these differences together is an opportunity to clarify core values and can lead to a better, shared understanding of the impact of the global pandemic.

We saw a large-scale response in the form of guaranteed annual income. The United States had a taste of how such a policy could work with the extraordinary financial support provided during the Covid-19 pandemic. People forced to stop working by the pandemic and the public health actions taken to combat it received more money than usual for unemployment insurance and received these amounts for an extended period. This money, combined with the pandemic's constant reminder of one's mortality, appeared to have generated major reflections about work for many people across sectors of the economy. It not only motivated them to consider other types of employment but gave them the financial support to explore alternatives. It was a sign that, without the absolute condition that one must work or starve, people became more reflective of their career aspirations and concerns for their well-being.

And indeed, the next large-scale response was "the great resignation," in which there was a high level of turnover across various industries. Records showed an unusual combination of high unemployment despite many job openings. Some people were leaving jobs, while many who were unemployed seemed reluctant to take on new jobs. It was also evident that issues differed between men and women, with women showing a greater reluctance to return to work.[4] One major reason for this is that homeschooling and child-care demands were abruptly ramped up during the pandemic, and women were more likely to have to deal with these new realities. These changes reflected a breakdown in the work infrastructure provided by schools and daycare services, which allowed parents to devote a large proportion of their time and energy to their jobs. Employers had been getting a free ride from that infrastructure, as it allowed people to devote more time and energy to their work than they could without that infrastructure—for which employers generally paid nothing.

Other factors contributed to this slow return to work. To some extent, the disruption of work life from the pandemic created opportunities for people to reflect on the job they had or used to have. For many, when they weighed their job in the balance, it came up wanting on important mismatches, such as control. With day-to-day life becoming more uncertain with shortages, shutdowns, and quarantines, people will shy away from jobs with rigid assignments and a lack of flexibility. For people who had been dealing with socially toxic workplace communities, the opportunity to work from home becomes a more appealing option than returning to a stressful set of colleagues.

Several organizations responded to "the great resignation" by offering extended breaks from work, such as regular "no-work" days or even a full week of company shutdown. As we saw in Chapter 4, on workload issues, the availability of vacations and breaks from work can be an important and welcomed coping technique. But if workers return from a break to the same mismatches of chronically stressful work conditions, then the benefit of the break will be very short term, and the risk of burnout will not have been prevented.

As we discussed earlier in this book, many workers have been facing the ongoing mantra that "The job is what it is, and you just have to adjust and keep up with it." But one of the important lessons learned from the pandemic is "The job does *not* have to be that way—things changed, and we had to figure out how to do the job differently." This is an important realization—jobs can be better—and so now people are looking for better opportunities, with better matches between themselves and the workplace.

Some Final Thoughts

In a work world where productivity is the important thing, we are proposing that human fulfillment should also be an important thing. What if, in addition to a living wage, the workplace provided its workers with the opportunity to realize satisfaction, happiness, and support for a meaningful life? What if, in addition to paying attention to the economic bottom line, we considered employees as carefully? The Declaration of Independence, which was the rationale for the founding of the United States, spoke about three unalienable rights given to all humans by their creator, which governments are supposed to protect: life, liberty, and the pursuit of happiness. What if we could be newly inspired by these ideals to reimagine better models for the world of work?

And what better time to develop a better model than now—when concerns about burnout have reached an all-time high, and the world of work has been disrupted by the Covid-19 pandemic? It might seem a bit crazy, or counterintuitive, to call for workplace change during a crisis—after all, shouldn't we stick with what we already know and do? Given that there has already been so much change and disruption, however, the opportunities are there for all of us to think outside of the box and to experiment with new procedures and alternative strategies.

The bottom line on burnout is that it is a social phenomenon, not an individual weakness. Interpersonal and organizational solutions need to be framed in terms of "we" and "us"—a sociocentric view rather than the "I" and "me" of an egocentric one—and they need to be shared and reciprocated by everyone. After the physical social distancing that was required to deal with Covid-19, we must now come together in a psychological partnership for the common good, so that we help all people achieve better health and well-being, both at work and at home. Our overall goal should be to design better job environments that will produce better job outcomes at all levels. When the *relationship* between workers and their workplace is functioning well, then the former will thrive, and the latter will succeed—truly a win-win situation.

Appendix

Assessing Your Own Relationship with Work

Instructions

In each of the six areas, how does your current job fit with your preferences, work patterns, and aspirations?

- If things on a given dimension are just right, put a check in the Just Right column.
- If a certain dimension is incompatible with your preferred way of working, put a check in the Mismatch column.
- If a quality is a major departure from your ideals, put a check in the Major Mismatch column.

Workload

	Just Right	Mismatch	Major Mismatch	Σ
Rating	0	1	2	Σ

The level of demands on
my time.

How frequently I take on
new tasks.

The frequency of
unanticipated incidents.

How often others
interrupt my flow.

The number of texts and
emails I must manage.

Workload Total

Control

	Just Right	Mismatch	Major Mismatch	Σ
Rating	0	1	2	Σ

The amount of
collaboration.

The amount of group
decision-making.

The balance of my
authority with my
responsibilities.

Calls upon my profes-
sional judgment.

My opportunities to show
initiative.

Control Total

Rewards			
	Just Right	Mismatch	Major Mismatch	
Rating	0	1	2	Σ

My pay and benefits.

Appreciation from others.

My opportunities for satisfying work.

My potential for promotion.

How often I can achieve a sense of flow at work.

Rewards Total

Community			
	Just Right	Mismatch	Major Mismatch	
Rating	0	1	2	Σ

Feeling psychologically safe at work.

The reliability of my colleagues.

The frequency of respectful social encounters.

The amount of time I work around other people.

The frequency of online, virtual meetings.

Community Total

Fairness			
Just Right	Mismatch	Major Mismatch	
Rating 0	1	2	Σ

The fairness of management decisions.

Allocation of resources to work groups.

The procedures for registering complaints with HR.

Work group civility.

Respect for diversity at work.

Fairness Total

Values			
Just Right	Mismatch	Major Mismatch	
Rating 0	1	2	Σ

The appropriateness of workplace values.

The salience of organizational values for me.

Management's commitment to its stated values.

The potential of my work to further what I care about.

The organization's impact on the environment.

Values Total

Notes

Introduction

1. J. Rothwell and S. Crabtree, "Not Just a Job: New Evidence on the Quality of Work in the United States," Gallup, October 20, 2019, https://www.gallup.com/education/267650/great-jobs-lumina-gates-omidyar-gallup-quality-download-report-2019.aspx.

2. Gallup, *State of the Global Workplace* (New York: Gallup Press, 2021).

3. A. Bryson and G. MacKerron, "Are You Happy While You Work?" *Economic Journal* 127, no. 599 (2017): 106–125.

4. H. Selye, *The Stress of Life* (New York: McGraw-Hill, 1956).

5. G. Greene, *A Burnt-Out Case* (London: Heinemann, 1961).

6. C. Maslach, "Burned-out," *Human Behavior* 9, no. 5 (1976): 16–22; C. Maslach, *Burnout: The Cost of Caring* (Englewood Cliffs, NJ: Prentice-Hall, 1982).

7. C. Maslach and M. P. Leiter, *The Truth about Burnout* (San Francisco: Jossey-Bass, 1997).

8. "Burnout an 'Occupational Phenomenon': International Classification of Diseases," World Health Organization, May 28, 2019, https://www.who.int/news/item/28-05-2019-burn-out-an-occupational-phenomenon-international-classification-of-diseases.

9. J. Pfeffer, *Dying for a Paycheck: How Modern Management Harms Employee Health and Company Performance—and What We Can Do about It* (New York: HarperCollins, 2018).

Chapter 1: Working in the Burnout Shop

1. Rachel Feintzeig, "Feeling Burned Out at Work? Join the Club," *Wall Street Journal*, February 28, 2017.

2. A. Spurgeon, J. M. Harrington, and C. L. Cooper, "Health and Safety Problems Associated with Long Working Hours: A Review of the Current Position," *Occupational and Environmental Medicine* 54, no. 6 (1997): 367–375.

3. N. K. Semmer, F. Tschan, L. L. Meier, S. Facchin, and N. Jacobshagen, "Illegitimate Tasks and Counterproductive Work Behavior," *Applied Psychology* 59, no. 1 (2010): 70–96.

4. T. Henderson, "In Most States, a Spike in 'Super Commuters,'" Stateline, Pew Charitable Trusts, June 5, 2017, https://www.pewtrusts.org/en/research-and-analysis/blogs/stateline/2017/06/05/in-most-states-a-spike-in-super-commuters.

5. C. Maslach and S. E. Jackson, "Lawyer Burn-out," *Barrister* 5, no. 2 (1978): 8.

6. Quote in "Burnout: Bertram Gawronski's Perspective," in L. M. Jaremka, J. M. Ackerman, B. Gawronski, et al., "Common Academic Experiences No One Talks About: Repeated Rejection, Imposter Syndrome, and Burnout," *Perspectives on Psychological Science* 15, no. 3 (2020): 519–543, 534.

7. T. Sharot, "What Motivates Employees More: Rewards or Punishments?" *Harvard Business Review*, September 26, 2017.

8. C. Purpora, M. A. Blegen, and N. A. Stotts, "Horizontal Violence among Hospital Staff Nurses Related to Oppressed Self or Oppressed Group," *Journal of Professional Nursing* 28, no. 5 (2012): 306–314.

9. M. E. Gomes, "The Rewards and Stresses of Social Change: A Qualitative Study of Peace Activists," *Journal of Humanistic Psychology* 32 (1992): 138–146.

10. C. Maslach and M. E. Gomes, "Overcoming Burnout," in *Working for Peace: A Handbook of Practical Psychology and Other Tools*, ed. R. M. McNair, 43–49 (Atascadero CA: Impact, 2006), 44.

11. Cheryl Biswas and Joshua Corman, interview by Matt Stephenson, "Hacking Our Way from Vicious-to-Virtuous Cycle," ThreatVector blog, BlackBerry, February 28, 2020, https://threatvector.cylance.com/en_us/home/video-cheryl-biswas-and-joshua-corman-hacking-our-way-from-vicious-to-virtuous-cycle.html.

12. J. A. Hollands, *Red Ink Behaviors* (Mountain View, CA: Blake / Madsen, 1997).

13. C. Goldin and C. Rouse, "Orchestrating Impartiality: The Impact of 'Blind' Auditions on Female Musicians," NBER Working Paper no. 5903, National Bureau of Economic Research, Cambridge MA, January 1997.

14. C. Goldin, "A Grand Gender Convergence: Its Last Chapter," *American Economic Review* 104, no. 4 (2014): 1091–1119.

15. Case study cited in M. Sacks, "Physician, Heal Thyself," *Stanford Magazine,* Stanford Alumni Association (May 2018): 28–29.

16. R. A. Karasek and T. Theorell, *Healthy Work: Stress, Productivity and the Reconstruction of Working Life* (New York: Basic Books, 1990).

17. C. Maslach, *Burnout: The Cost of Caring* (Englewood Cliffs, NJ: Prentice-Hall, 1982).

18. A. B. Bakker, P. M. LeBlanc, and W. B. Schaufeli, "Burnout Contagion among Intensive Care Nurses," *Journal of Advanced Nursing* 51 (2005): 276–287.

19. A. Jameton, "Dilemmas of Moral Distress: Moral Responsibility and Nursing Practice," *AWHONNS Clinical Issues in Perinatal and Women's Health Nursing* 4, no. 4 (1993): 542–551.

20. A. Montgomery, "Covid-19 and the Problem of Employee Silence in Healthcare," BMJ Opinion blog, June 23, 2020, https://blogs.bmj.com/bmj /2020/06/23/covid-19-and-the-problem-of-employee-silence-in-healthcare /?utm_campaign=shareaholic&utm_medium=twitter&utm_source=social network.

Chapter 2: Sounding the Alarm

1. Quoted in C. Maslach, *Burnout: The Cost of Caring* (Englewood Cliffs, NJ: Prentice-Hall, 1982), 8.

2. C. Maslach and S. E. Jackson, "The Measurement of Experienced Burnout," *Journal of Occupational Behavior* 2 (1981): 99–113. The MBI is a copyrighted measure that is published and distributed by Mind Garden, a publisher of psychological tests: C. Maslach, S. E. Jackson, M. P. Leiter, W. B. Schaufeli, and R. L. Schwab, *Maslach Burnout Inventory Manual,* 4th ed. (Menlo Park, CA: Mind Garden, 2017). Complete information about the psychometric development and use of the MBI is contained in the MBI Manual.

3. C. Maslach and S. E. Jackson, *MBI: Human Services Survey* (Menlo Park, CA: Mind Garden, 1981).

4. John Willis, "Karōjisatsu: Death from Overwork," *IT Revolution Blog,* February 27, 2015, https://itrevolution.com/karojisatsu/.

5. P. F. Hewlin, "And the Award Goes To . . . : Facades of Conformity in Organizational Settings," *Academy of Management Review* 28, no. 4 (2003): 633–642.

6. A. R. Hochschild, *The Managed Heart: Commercialization of Human Feeling* (Berkeley: University of California Press, 1983).

7. "Burnout an 'Occupational Phenomenon': International Classification of Diseases," World Health Organization, May 28, 2019, https://www.who.int /news/item/28-05-2019-burn-out-an-occupational-phenomenon-international -classification-of-diseases.

8. A. Frances, letter, *New Yorker,* June 14, 2021, 5.

9. American Psychological Association, "Building Your Resilience," APA Psychology Topics, January 1, 2012, updated February 1, 2020, https://www.apa .org/topics/resilience; I. T. Robertson, C. L. Cooper, M. Sarkar, and T. Curran, "Resilience Training in the Workplace from 2003 to 2014: A Systematic Review," *Journal of Occupational and Organizational Psychology* 88, no. 3 (2015): 533–562.

10. M. P. Leiter and C. Maslach, "Interventions to Prevent and Alleviate Burnout," in *Burnout at Work: A Psychological Perspective,* ed. M. P. Leiter, A. B. Bakker, and C. Maslach, 145–167 (New York: Psychology Press, 2014).

11. M. P. Leiter and C. Maslach, "Latent Burnout Profiles: A New Approach to Understanding the Burnout Experience," *Burnout Research* 3 (2016): 89–100.

12. M. P. Leiter and C. Maslach, *Areas of Worklife Scale Manual,* 5th ed. (Menlo Park, CA: Mind Garden, 2011); Maslach, Jackson, Leiter, Schaufeli, and Schwab, *Maslach Burnout Inventory Manual.*

13. W. Schaufeli and A. Bakker, "UWES Utrecht Work Engagement Scale," Preliminary Manual, Version 1, November 2003, Occupational Health Psychology Unit, Utrecht University.

14. J. K. Harter, T. L. Hayes, and F. L. Schmidt, "Meta-analytic Predictive Validity of Gallup Selection Research Instruments (SRI)," technical report, Gallup Organization, Omaha, NE, January 2004.

15. C. Maslach and M. P. Leiter, "Burnout: What It Is and How to Measure It," in *HBR Guide to Beating Burnout,* 211–221 (Boston: Harvard Business Review Press, 2020).

16. Leiter and Maslach, "Latent Burnout Profiles."

Chapter 3: Rethinking the Relationship between Person and Job

1. W. E. Deming, *The New Economics for Industry, Government, and Education* (Cambridge, MA: MIT Center for Advanced Engineering Study, 1993).

2. C. Maslach and C. G. Banks, "Psychological Connections with Work," in *The Routledge Companion to Wellbeing at Work*, ed. C. L. Cooper and M. P. Leiter, 37–54 (New York: Routledge, 2017).

3. R. M. Ryan and E. L. Deci, *Self-Determination Theory: Basic Psychological Needs in Motivation, Development, and Wellness* (New York: Guilford Press, 2017).

4. L. Ross and R. E. Nisbett, *The Person and the Situation* (New York: McGraw-Hill, 1991).

5. C. Maslach and S. E. Jackson, "Patterns of Burnout among a National Sample of Public Contact Workers," *Journal of Health and Human Resources Administration* 7, no. 2 (1984): 189–212.

6. C. G. Banks, "Collection of Critical Incidents: Identifying Organizational Features That Promote or Diminish Employee Health, Well-Being, and Productivity in Organizations," research tool, Interdisciplinary Center for Healthy Workplaces, University of California, Berkeley; L. D. Butterfield, W. A. Borgen, N. E. Amundson, and A. T. Maglio, "Fifty Years of the Critical Incident Technique: 1954–2004 and Beyond," *Qualitative Research* 5, no. 4 (2005): 475–497.

7. E. Seppälä, *The Happiness Track: How to Apply the Science of Happiness to Accelerate Your Success* (New York: HarperCollins, 2016).

Chapter 4: Workload

1. B. S. Asgari, P. Pickar, and V. Garay, "Karoshi and Karo-jisatsu in Japan: Causes, Statistics and Prevention Mechanisms," *Asia Pacific Business and Economics Perspectives* 4, no. 2 (2016): 49–72.

2. C. Weller, "Japan Is Facing a 'Death by Overwork' Problem—Here's What It's All About," *BusinessInsider*, October 18, 2017.

3. H. Hwang, W. M. Hur, and Y. Shin, "Emotional Exhaustion among the South Korean Workforce before and after COVID-19," *Psychology and Psychotherapy: Theory, Research and Practice* 94, no. 2 (2021): 371–381.

4. M. Drillinger, "The Tired Generation: 4 Reasons Millennials Are Always Exhausted," Healthline, March 29, 2020, https://www.healthline.com /health/millennials-exhausted-all-the-time.

5. Eight Hour Day Monument, Russell and Victoria Streets, Melbourne, https://citycollection.melbourne.vic.gov.au/eight-hour-day-memorial/.

6. Quoted in C. Maslach, *Burnout: The Cost of Caring* (Englewood Cliffs, NJ: Prentice-Hall, 1982), 110.

7. J. O'Connell, "Burnout Left Me on the Floor, Unable to Move," *Irish Times Magazine,* September 16, 2017, 12.

8. H. Davidson, "'Touching Fish' Craze Sees China's Youth Find Ways to Laze amid '996' Work Culture," *Guardian,* January 22, 2021.

9. P. F. DeChant, A. Acs, K. B. Rhee, T. S. Boulanger, J. L. Snowdon, M. A. Tutty, C. A. Sinsky, and K. J. T. Craig, "Effect of Organization-Directed Workplace Interventions on Physician Burnout: A Systematic Review," *Mayo Clinic Proceedings: Innovations, Quality and Outcomes* 3, no. 4 (2019): 384–408.

10. Medscape, "'Death by 1000 Cuts': Medscape National Physician Burnout and Suicide Report," 2021.

11. M. Valcour, "Beating Burnout," *Harvard Business Review* 94, no. 11 (2016): 98–101.

12. Maslach, *Burnout.*

13. S. Sonnentag and C. Fritz, "The Recovery Experience Questionnaire: Development and Validation of a Measure for Assessing Recuperation and Unwinding from Work," *Journal of Occupational Health Psychology* 12, no. 3 (2007): 204–221.

14. T. Shlain, *24 / 6: The Power of Unplugging One Day a Week* (New York: Simon and Schuster, 2019), xii.

15. O'Connell, "Burnout Left Me on the Floor."

Chapter 5: Control

1. D. McGregor, *The Human Side of Enterprise* (New York: McGraw-Hill, 1960).

2. Price Waterhouse Cooper, "It's Time to Reimagine Where and How Work Will Get Done," PwC's US Remote Work Survey, January 12, 2021, https://www.pwc.com/us/en/library/covid-19/us-remote-work-survey.html.

3. C. Merrill, "As a CEO, I Worry about the Erosion of Office Culture with More Remote Work," *Washington Post,* May 6, 2021.

4. See, for example, tweet by Andrew Beaujon @abeaujon, May 7, 2021.

5. C. Brown and T. Wond, "Building Career Mobility: A Critical Exploration of Career Capital," *Journal of the National Institute for Career Education and Counselling* 41, no. 1 (2018): 56–63.

6. J. McWhinney, "The Demise of the Defined-Benefit Plan," Investopedia, updated November 28, 2021, https://www.investopedia.com/articles/retirement/06/demiseofdbplan.asp.

Chapter 6: Rewards

1. J. Siegrist, "Adverse Health Effects of High-Effort/Low-Reward Conditions," *Journal of Occupational Health Psychology* 1, no. 1 (1996): 27–41; K. Hyvönen, T. Feldt, K. Salmela-Aro, U. Kinnunen, and A. Mäkikangas, "Young Managers' Drive to Thrive: A Personal Work Goal Approach to Burnout and Work Engagement," *Journal of Vocational Behavior* 75, no. 2 (2009): 183–196.

2. D. B. Morris and E. L. Usher, "Developing Teaching Self-Efficacy in Research Institutions: A Study of Award-Winning Professors," *Contemporary Educational Psychology* 36, no. 3 (2011): 232–245.

3. C. Newport, *Deep Work: Rules for Focused Success in a Distracted World* (New York: Grand Central, 2016).

Chapter 7: Community

1. L. M. Andersson and C. M. Pearson, "Tit for Tat? The Spiraling Effect of Incivility in the Workplace," *Academy of Management Review* 24, no. 3 (1999): 452–471, 454.

2. E. H. Schein, "Organizational Culture," *American Psychologist* 45, no. 2 (1990): 109–119.

3. W. Hernandez, A. Luthanen, D. Ramsel, and K. Osatuke, "The Mediating Relationship of Self-Awareness on Supervisor Burnout and Workgroup Civility and Psychological Safety: A Multilevel Path Analysis," *Burnout Research* 2, no. 1 (2015): 36–49.

4. M. R. Tuckey, A. B. Bakker, and M. F. Dollard, "Empowering Leaders Optimize Working Conditions for Engagement: A Multilevel Study," *Journal of Occupational Health Psychology* 17, no. 1 (2012): 15–27.

5. C. L. Chullen, "How Does Supervisor Burnout Affect Leader-Member Exchange? A Dyadic Perspective," *International Business and Economics Research Journal* 13, no. 5 (2014): 1113–1126.

6. M. P. Leiter, "Assessment of Workplace Social Encounters: Social Profiles, Burnout, and Engagement," *International Journal of Environmental Research and Public Health* 18, no. 7 (2021), 3533.

7. M. P. Leiter, H. K. S. Laschinger, A. Day, and D. Gilin-Oore, "The Impact of Civility Interventions on Employee Social Behavior, Distress, and Attitudes," *Journal of Applied Psychology* 96, no. 6 (2011): 1258–1274.

8. M. P. Leiter, A. Day, D. Gilin-Oore, and H. K. S. Laschinger, "Getting Better and Staying Better: Assessing Civility, Incivility, Distress and Job

Attitudes One Year after a Civility Intervention," *Journal of Occupational Health Psychology* 17, no. 4 (2012): 425–434.

9. M. van Dijke, D. De Cremer, D. M. Mayer, and N. Van Quaquebeke, "When Does Procedural Fairness Promote Organizational Citizenship Behavior? Integrating Empowering Leadership Types in Relational Justice Models," *Organizational Behavior and Human Decision Processes* 117, no. 2 (2012): 235–248.

Chapter 8: Fairness

1. M. P. Leiter, H. K. S. Laschinger, A. Day, and D. Gilin-Oore, "The Impact of Civility Interventions on Employee Social Behavior, Distress, and Attitudes," *Journal of Applied Psychology* 96, no. 6 (2011): 1258–1274.

2. C. Maslach and M. P. Leiter, "Early Predictors of Job Burnout and Engagement," *Journal of Applied Psychology* 93, no. 3 (2008): 498–512.

3. A. Montgomery, E. Panagopoulou, A. Esmail, T. Richards, and C. Maslach, "Burnout in Healthcare: The Case for Organizational Change," *BMJ* 366 (2019): l4774 (1–5).

Chapter 9: Values

1. B. Allyn, "Google Workers Speak Out about Why They Formed a Union: 'To Protect Ourselves,'" *Morning Edition,* NPR, January 8, 2021, https://www .npr.org/2021/01/08/954710407/at-google-hundreds-of-workers-formed-a -labor-union-why-to-protect-ourselves.

2. C. Maslach and M. P. Leiter, *The Truth about Burnout* (San Francisco: Jossey-Bass, 1997).

3. A. M. Carton, "'I'm Not Mopping the Floors, I'm Putting a Man on the Moon': How NASA Leaders Enhanced the Meaningfulness of Work by Changing the Meaning of Work," *Administrative Science Quarterly* 63, no. 2 (2018): 323–369.

4. G. P. Shultz, "Trust Is the Coin of the Realm," Hoover Institution, December 11, 2020, https://www.hoover.org/research/trust-coin-realm.

5. M. Valcour, "Beating Burnout," *Harvard Business Review* 94, no. 11 (2016): 98–101.

Chapter 10: Creating Better Matches

1. Maslach Burnout Toolkit (MBI and AWS): C. Maslach, S. E. Jackson, M. P. Leiter, W. B. Schaufeli, and R. L. Schwab, "Maslach Burnout Inventory,"

2016; and M. P. Leiter and C. Maslach, "Areas of Worklife Survey," 2000, Mind Garden Press, https://www.mindgarden.com/184-maslach-burnout-toolkit.

2. M. P. Leiter and C. Maslach, *Banishing Burnout: Six Strategies for Improving Your Relationship with Work* (San Francisco: Jossey-Bass, 2005).

3. We borrow the term "99 percent invisible" from Roman Mars, who hosts a podcast by that title (http://99percentinvisible.org/). For a classic argument for "invisible" design, also see Don Norman, *The Design of Everyday Things: Revised and Expanded Edition* (New York: Basic Books, 2013).

4. S. Trzeciak, B. W. Roberts, and A. J. Mazzarelli, "Compassionomics: Hypothesis and Experimental Approach," *Medical Hypotheses* 107 (2017): 92–97.

Chapter 11: Making Matches Work

1. M. Leiter, "SCORE (Strengthening a Culture of Respect and Engagement) Overview," WorkEngagement, January 8, 2020, https://mpleiter.com/2020/01/08/score-strengthening-a-culture-of-respect-and-engagement-overview/.

2. "Bullying and Harassment in the Health Sector," Victorian Auditor-General's Report, PP No. 148, Melbourne, Victoria, Australia, March 2016, https://www.audit.vic.gov.au/sites/default/files/20160323-Bullying.pdf. Quote on 12.

3. M. P. Leiter, *Social Encounters Scale Manual* (Menlo Park, CA: Mind Garden Press, 2019).

4. C. Maslach, S. E. Jackson, M. P. Leiter, W. B. Schaufeli, and R. L. Schwab, *Maslach Burnout Inventory Manual,* 4th ed. (Menlo Park, CA: Mind Garden, 2017).

Chapter 12: Meeting the Challenge of Burnout

1. "Will Workers Return to the Office?" *Economist,* June 6, 2021.

2. J. Useem, "The Psychological Benefits of Commuting to Work," *Atlantic* (July/August 2021).

3. L. Fessler, "Workplace Harassment in the Age of Remote Work," *New York Times,* June 8, 2021.

4. "Seven Charts That Show Covid-19's Impact on Women's Employment," McKinsey and Company report, March 8, 2021, https://www.mckinsey.com/featured-insights/diversity-and-inclusion/seven-charts-that-show-covid-19s-impact-on-womens-employment.

Acknowledgments

We first wrote a book about burnout twenty-five years ago, writing on opposite ends of the North American continent and using the new technology of email to send immediate revisions back and forth. Now we have repeated that process again, but this time as we sheltered in place during an unbelievable and still unfolding global pandemic that has changed the world of work. We hope that a clear understanding of what burnout is, why it happens, and what we can do about it will provide some valuable lessons to guide us to a better future.

Our special thanks go to the people who helped create and carry on the indispensable use of the Maslach Burnout Inventory over four decades, to discover ever more about burnout: Harrison Gough, Susan E. Jackson, and Robb Most; to Paola Coda, who designed the visual images to enhance our words; and to Janice Audet, whose invitation to write this book, and subsequent feedback along the way, has made it possible.

Index

ʃ

psychological safety: addressing community mismatch and, 208, 211; community
match and, 181; person-job match and,
65; social support and establishing, 139
public restrooms, equity and design of,
149

reciprocal trust, 165–166
reciprocity: fairness and, 145–149;
generating change and power of,
208–209; in interpersonal workplace
dynamics, 146–147; modeling civility
and, 221
recognition: fostering community and,
124–126; multiple forms of, 126–127;
sources of, 119
recovery, from workload, 87, 88–91
redesign of mismatches, 78–80, 187–195;
building in progress checkpoints,
191–195; design guidelines, 188–191;
internal and external resources and,
194–195; recognizing good design,
187–188. *See also* design
"red-ink behavior," 22
relaxation strategies, as coping technique,
49
remote communications, ground rules
for, 229
remote work: boundaries between work
and nonwork and, 96; control and,
105–106; downside of, 228–229; finding
social support and, 141–142, 143; flexibility and, 112–113; job security and,
106–107; mutual trust and, 99; on-site
work mixed with, 227, 228; pandemic
and, 219, 226–229; productivity and,
226–227; supervision and, 109
resilience, 48; work, pandemic, and, 225
resources and assets: to manage workplace change, 194–195; outcomes and
results *vs.*, 148–149
respect: civility and, 131; fairness and,
145–149; mutual, 130; rewards and, 121;
trust and, 166. *See also* Strengthening a
Culture of Respect and Engagement
(SCORE)

rewards, 116–127; appreciation, 118–119;
compensation system, 116–117; credibility and rewards system design,
117–118; extrinsic rewards, 120–124;
fairness and assignment of, 150–154;
gratifying recognition and, 74; inherent
in the work, 118; insufficient, 6, 18–20;
intrinsic rewards, 124–127; social,
19–20; social dimension of work and,
26; social domain and, 218; supervisory relationships and, 115
rhythm, redesign of better matches and
work-life, 190–191, 192–193
role-plays, Strengthening a Culture
of Respect and Engagement, 208,
209
rules and regulations, autonomy and,
108–109

schedules, lack of control over work, 17
Schultz, George, 165
self-awareness, coping with stress and
raising, 49
self-care, individual approach to burnout
and, 220
self-determination theory, 64
self-efficacy in one's job, 35
self-evaluation of efficacy, 52. 57
self-evaluation on the job, burnout and,
52
self-serving bias, extrinsic rewards and,
120
Seppälä, Emma, 81–82
service overtime, 85–86
shared care, protecting personal time
and, 220
Shlain, Tiffany, 97
Silicon Valley workplaces, as "burnout
shops," 4, 11, 15
Sisyphus, 13
situational attributions, focus on context
and, 67
situational context, burnout and, 59–60
situational factors in lack of control,
16–17
skepticism about workplace change, 199